FOSTERING
Hope

FOSTERING
Hope

THE STORY OF CROSSROADS HOPE ACADEMY

By

John M. Davidson, M.Ed.

XULON PRESS

Xulon Press
2301 Lucien Way #415
Maitland, FL 32751
407.339.4217
www.xulonpress.com

Edited by Deb Hall at TheWrightInsight.com (Deb@TheWrightInsight.com)
Cover design by Ruth Deal

Paperback ISBN-13: 978-1-66284-953-4
Ebook ISBN-13: 978-1-66284-954-1

To God be the glory.
(2 Corinthians 3:5)

Hope deferred makes the heart sick, but a longing
fulfilled is a tree of life.

—Proverbs 13:12 (NIV)

TABLE OF CONTENTS

Acknowledgments

I'm dedicating this book to my late mother, Charlotte Davidson, who taught me to always finish what I start. She once told me a story about an author she met who told her that most people intend to write a book but very few ever finish one. The conversation motivated her to finish her book on the history of the Girl Scouts. Her gift of that story has motivated me to finish this book.

I'd like to thank my wife for her encouragement to finish this work and for her tireless editing. When I met her, she was already a published author, and I'm grateful for her ability to help guide me through to completion of this book.

I'd like also to thank our staff and board members. I have learned so much through the years by watching you solve problems. I am in the fortunate (and at times unfortunate) position of being the face of Crossroads Hope Academy, but you are the real reason our organization exists and thrives.

Crossroads Hope Academy began with a mission to help kids find their way, to be that beacon of hope and stability, the firm but loving foundation every kid deserves. We have learned so much since we took those first tentative steps into the world of foster care. Our vision of what could be has grown with each passing year, and we are grateful for the many dozens of tireless volunteers who have selflessly walked this journey with us. With your continued support, we will continue to provide a safe and caring atmosphere for the vulnerable population we serve.

One hundred percent of the proceeds from this book will return back to the mission that I so love 96.8 percent of the time.

Introduction

There are many variables working against foster kids, and no one person or entity has control over much of it. There are the families that are fractured and plagued with drug abuse, mental illness, ignorance, or some evil influence. There are the first responders, the child protective investigators who are often right out of college, young and inexperienced, who are idealistic but lack the practical understanding gained by time in the field. Not many of them stick around; they leave with PTSD or transfer to a job that isn't on the front lines; or worse, they become callous to the plight of the families they are working with. Then you have the court system, which operates from a not-so-complex system of rules to govern an infinitely complex human dynamic problem. There are caseworkers who have giant caseloads and typically burn out after a year and a half. The caseworkers arguably have the most information about each of their kids than any other person in the foster care system. So, when they leave their post after a year or two, and another comes in to try to understand a kid who has been in the system for ten years, there are obviously a lot of gaps. Finally, there are the foster caregivers, whose sense of normal is much different from their charges. In many cases the foster "parents" can't or won't handle the behaviors of their foster child. That is why in the United States, foster kids average three different placements, which in itself is traumatic.

I don't want to discourage you. In fact, my goal in writing this book is to encourage you to get involved with the foster care system. My experience has shown me that most people have very little knowledge about foster care. The United States has almost a half million kids in foster care and exponentially fewer people willing to help care for them. After reading this book, I hope your eyes are opened but at the same time your fears, diminished. My hope is that you will be informed and motivated to get involved.

SECTION I

Preliminary Stuff You Might Want to Know

Chapter 1

A Very Brief History of Foster Care

Brandon

At his monthly treatment team meeting, Brandon told the staff that his dad was going to court the next day and that he would be going home with him the following week. Brandon had been with us for eight months after spending the past ten years in fifteen different foster homes while both of his parents went in and out of jail for various drug crimes. The following Sunday after our meeting, Brandon sat on the edge of our dirt road all day long. He came in to use the phone three times to call his dad, but his dad didn't pick up. Brandon then used a friend's phone to call his dad, who picked up but then quickly hung up when he heard Brandon's voice. On Monday our case manager, Charity, had the unenviable position of letting Brandon know that his dad never went to court last week and that the judge terminated his parental rights. Brandon was inconsolable. At the young age of thirteen, he had to come to grips with the fact that he would never be going home. Later that night, Brandon threatened suicide and spent three days in the crisis stabilization unit.

Upon return, Brandon came to our business manager, Ms. Tina, and told her that he was able to talk to his dad, who told him he had been outside the courtroom in the hallway but the judge never called him in to hear his case. Brandon cautiously asked, "Do you think he was telling the truth, Ms. Tina?" Tina told him that the judge had to make his decision publicly in front a lot of adults. She asked Brandon if he thought the judge would be able to lie in that situation. "I didn't think my dad was telling the truth" was his response.

Foster care has been around as long as there have been families. Since the beginning of time, villages and small communities would absorb the work of caring for a child whose parents became missing in action. The history of the institution of foster care in North America can be traced back to Jamestown in 1636. The settlers enacted the English Poor Law of 1562 for a seven-year-old boy named Benjamin Eaton.

The English Poor Law basically allowed wealthy families to take in poor or orphaned kids and subjugate them to indentured servitude until they became of age. This practice is still very common in many places around the world.

In 1853 Charles Loring Brace began a program for orphans that would become iconic in the history of the foster care system in the United States. In the late nineteenth century and early twentieth century, there was a large population of homeless children in the Northeast due to poverty and a massive influx of immigrants. Many of the street kids would take to theft and even prostitution to support themselves.

Pastor Brace and the organization that he founded, the Children's Aid Society, would pick kids up off the streets of New York and place them on trains heading to places throughout the country. It is estimated that between 1853 and 1930 more than 120,000 kids rode those "orphan trains" and found new homes, predominantly in the Midwest.

Although well intentioned, the glaring issue was that the foster homes were not prescreened, so the safety of those kids was in question. Additionally, only about 50 percent of the kids in the project were actually orphans, and questions arose about kids being relocated simply because of someone's opinion of what was best for them. Many families who took the kids in, especially the older kids, did so because they needed labor to work the farms.

Another big controversy with Brace's program was that most of the relocated kids were from Italian, Irish, or Polish families. Pastor Brace was criticized for sending them to predominantly Protestant families and accused of trying to ethnically cleanse the city. Interestingly, a large number of the older kids who were emigrated on the orphan trains ran away from their placements. Kids running away from their foster placements continues to be a problem in the foster care system more than a hundred years later.

In 1885 Pennsylvania became the first state to pass a law requiring all foster homes to become licensed. In 1935 the federal government passed the Social Security Act providing funding for foster families and required home inspections by the states before foster placement. As of the date of this writing, about 50% of funding for foster care comes to the individual states from the federal government.

In 2018 the Families First Prevention Services Act (FFPSA) passed. It was initially shot down in Washington several years in a row before it was slid into law with the Hurricane Matthew funding legislation. States scrambled as the FFPSA required new placement types and more restrictive placement criteria and required states to give more attention to how and where they were placing their foster kids. The FFPSA didn't fully take effect nationally until October 2021 and required group foster homes to identify as a certain type and meet the requirements of that type. Many of us in foster care don't like the inferences that the FFPSA makes regarding group living facilities because it presupposes that congregate care is not good for kids. By and large that is true, but some foster kids need exponentially more services than a normal household is able to provide. Those are the kids who come to places like Crossroads Hope Academy.

Prescriptively, kids are placed in group foster homes due to their behavioral and mental health needs. Sometimes, however, kids are placed in congregate care due to the lack of licensed single-family placements. Kids fail out of inappropriate placements, and as kids bounce from one to home the next, they become increasingly traumatized and, not surprisingly, more difficult to work with.

In 2014 I took two kids with me to go speak before our county's legislative delegation. After explaining to them that boys at our home on average had been to fourteen different foster placements, one senator told me that group foster homes were too expensive and the kids needed to be in "regular" homes. I was prepared to answer that objection because I knew her disposition and anticipated her remarks.

I reiterated the number of failed placements our kids had had, and that the behaviors they exhibited required far more services than a normal household could provide.

I quoted the USDA's cost figures for medical and mental health counseling as well as their estimates for raising a child in the current economy. I finished by illustrating that if a child of a single mother who had no insurance got cancer or lost a leg in an accident, no politician would decry the cost of her medical bills. However, when a foster kid, who looks outwardly normal, has life-debilitating and unseen trauma, why are they not treated similarly? She relented after I received an ovation from the audience for speaking what they knew all too well was the truth.

As recently as the 1970s, most states handed foster kids a bus ticket and a few hundred dollars when they turned eighteen and wished them luck. Can you imagine? Were you able to fend for yourself at that age? Were your kids able to? Currently, every state in the nation has some sort of provision for kids after they have aged out of the foster care system. In Florida, kids can get services and financial assistance until the age of twenty-two, with some provisions: they must work and/or go to school full-time. From my perspective, the number of foster kids who find themselves homeless or incarcerated not long after leaving the foster care system is still far too high.

There are 440,000 kids in foster care in the United States at the date of this writing. Over 23,000 in Florida alone. It is estimated that there are over 100,000,000 orphans worldwide. That number is staggering.

Some additional relevant statistics from the Casey Foundation (Casey.org):

- On average, foster kids are shuffled to three different placements while in foster care.

- One in four foster boys in the U.S. will be homeless by age twenty-two.

- One in five foster boys will be incarcerated by the age of twenty-two.

- 80 percent of adults in the adult corrections system are former foster children.

- 50 percent of foster girls will have had their first child by the age of twenty-two.

- Foster kids are five times more likely to attempt suicide.

- Less than 50 percent of foster kids get their high school diploma on time at the age of eighteen.

- Less than 2 percent of foster kids will attend college after getting their high school diploma.

More numbers from the National Foster Youth Institute (NFYI.org):

- After reaching the age of eighteen, 20 percent of foster youth will become instantly homeless.

- Only 50 percent of foster youth will have gainful employment by the age of twenty-four.

- Less than 3 percent of foster youth will earn a college degree at any point in their life.

- 25 percent of foster kids who age out of the system still suffer from Post-Traumatic Stress Disorder (PTSD).

- 25 percent of kids who age out of foster care will not be able to get their high school diploma or GED.

- 75 percent of women and 33 percent of men will receive government benefits to meet basic needs after aging out of foster care.

- 50 percent of kids aging out of the foster care system will develop a substance dependence.

A famous quote by Mark Twain offers, "There are three kinds of lies: lies, damned lies, and statistics."

While I agree with Mr. Twain and am often skeptical of numbers touted, for many people numbers are impactful, so I have chosen to include some of the more eye-opening statistics around foster care. For me, reading a single kid's case file and the atrocities that have happened to him over his life and then spending time with him far outweighs statistics. It is what motivates me to action.

Having said that, I have learned through the years that when I speak to groups about Crossroads and foster care in general, I always get gasps from the crowd when they hear some of the more disparaging statistics. If you are unfamiliar with foster care, I'm sure you may have a similar reaction.

The first group of numbers listed above represents the dismal outcomes that exist for foster kids once they age out. If you have a hard time believing them, just know that so did we when we first started in foster care as Crossroads Hope Academy. Over the years, however, we have witnessed the level of trauma endured by foster kids. Their trauma, combined with the instability of their living and schooling arrangements, raises the likelihood of their mental health and relational problems significantly.

I once had the missions board from a local church come for a tour of our campus. They were all retiree volunteers with the church. One of the men kept asking me about the Crossroads statistics juxtaposed against national statistics. He wanted to know what kind of success rate we had.

I gave him the Mark Twain quote about statistics and shared some of the reasoning about why I don't advertise them, but here are the current statistics about the forty-one boys who have turned eighteen and therefore aged out of Crossroads Hope Academy:

- Seven are in college or post-secondary vocational education.

- The majority have received their high school diploma.

- Two are incarcerated.

- Two are homeless.

- The majority of them are gainfully employed (a few also in school).

- Three now have their own children and a significant other.

While we are certainly proud that our efforts have resulted in beating the odds with many of our former foster kids, there is still so much more work to be done. When we first started this transition from juvenile justice to foster care, I don't think anyone involved imagined how challenging and rewarding that experience would prove to be.

We have a dream and a plan for how we'd like to see Crossroads Hope Academy evolve as we move forward. But coming from where we started is nothing less than a miracle, really. What follows is the story of the little foster home that could.

Chapter 2

Motivation to Grow

Josh

J osh had been to fifty-two different foster placements in eight counties in Florida before he came to Crossroads. At sixteen, he was very street savvy and, although far behind in school, very intelligent. Josh was an established loner, though. The relationships he established with other boys and adults were superficial. One of our local benefactors decided he and his wife would mentor Josh and spend time with him off campus. They got their background checks and other foster care requirements completed just in time for his birthday to bring Josh to their house so he could have a homemade birthday supper with them. When the wife asked Josh what he would like for his birthday dinner, Josh replied he had never chosen his meals before—not just for his birthday, but for any meal! The couple was blown away and called me immediately after their night with him was over. I explained that at fifty-two foster placements, it is likely he had never even been inside the kitchen of one of his placement homes, let alone chosen what he wanted to eat.

Josh told the couple some excessively tall tales, which they questioned me about. I explained that I had not completely cracked the code on the extravagant lies it seemed many of our foster kids told, but I was sure there was a solid link to self-esteem there somewhere. I advised them not to take everything he said at face value and only give attention to the things they could verify. We worked with him on the other side, reminding him that trust and truthfulness are foundational for all relationships. For a kid who had no relationships, this was not so obvious a code.

After Josh had been with us for just over six months, he hit a wall of depression culminating in him not getting out of bed for over a week and ultimately causing us to have to transfer him to a therapeutic foster home for his own safety. Before we moved him, though, I planted a seed while talking with him. I asked him to tell me how many case managers he had had in his foster career. "Ten," he told me. How many family court judges? "Four." He couldn't tell me how many schools he had attended or neighborhoods he had lived in. "Josh," I asked him, "you have moved around so much in your life and have been through so many relationships that no one actually knows you! It's fair to say that after knowing you for only six months, I know you better than anyone on the planet, and that's not good!" He agreed, but he didn't really value the magnitude of the fact as much as I did.

Josh contacted me on social media a year after leaving us. I'm hopeful that my words haunted him into valuing stability more than running from his problems. He also contacted his mentor (my volunteer) and wanted all of us to know that he was working and appreciated everything we had done for him. Contacting us demonstrated the value he placed on our relationship, but showing his appreciation demonstrated a higher level of maturity, which made us proud. Unfortunately, at the date of this writing, we have not heard from Josh for more than five years.

When I give tours or talk to service clubs or churches, the questions that I receive lead me to believe most people don't know there are radical differences between the motivations of a foster kid and those of a kid raised in a "normal" setting. Most adults remember Abraham Maslow, so I often use his Hierarchy of Needs theory as a backdrop to help them understand why we have so many challenges raising foster kids. This discussion has also been instrumental in helping policy makers understand why they should place more value on stability for foster children.

Abraham Maslow, as you may remember from freshman psychology, theorized that humans motivate under a hierarchy of needs. A person cannot move to the next level of need, or the motivations it allows, until the current need is met. Notice his chart below:

At the very bottom of the pyramid is physiological needs: food, water, and shelter *for today*. According to Maslow, if you do not know where your physiological needs can be met *for today*, you will care truly little, if at all, about your family and friends, your job, or your education. You are in survival mode. Once your physical needs are met *for today*, your next motivation is to prepare to take care of yourself for subsequent days, weeks, or months (this is your need for safety). At the point where your stability is satisfied, then you begin to take care of your relationships and to value friendships. This is where my social science lesson is going to stop so I can get back to talking about my boys. Keep in mind, however, things like money, status, education, and recognition fall in the esteem category, and we don't seek those things until we are fulfilled in the social (or relational) category.

If a foster kid has had twenty different foster placements in his fifteen years of life, he doesn't know anyone. Our boys come to Crossroads assuming they will be able to eat and sleep, but they have no idea when or where. In effect, they are in survival mode, or at best, safety mode, when they come through our doors for the first time. Even if they slide up into the next rung of the hierarchy, they have been bounced around enough to know they could be moved at any moment and so do not grasp the stability quickly that would let them advance to the social (i.e., love and belonging) rung of Maslow's hierarchy. We sometimes see our boys sit in this spot for months before they buckle down in their education.

Once the kid finally moves into the social rung of the hierarchy, it can take a long time to see his behaviors become less erratic. Relationships take time to develop, and there is no shortcutting. This is why we will witness new kids Baker-Act themselves (threaten suicide so they will be taken to a Crisis Stabilization Unit, or CSU) when they are clearly not suicidal. For them, there are no consequences for threatening to hurt themselves, only benefits: they put themselves in a position of power and control, they get a break from the scenery, there are girls at the CSU, and they have no responsibilities there.

Baker-Acting oneself should be as foreign of a concept to you as it was to me. When I was in ninth grade, if I would have pretended to hurt myself to get a little extra attention, my friends would have disassociated themselves from me. But what if a person does not have any friends or relationships? As a point of probable interest, we don't often have kids Baker-Act themselves who are truly depressed or suicidal, and of course we take every kid seriously when he makes the threat. However, spending twenty-four hours per day with them, we know who is playing games much like you would with your own child.

If you grew up in any "normal" family situation, you had (have) at least one relationship in which, no matter what, you were (are) accepted as you are. For example, I know that my dad would have never visited me in jail had I found myself there. He told me so. However, he would not have disowned me, no matter what I did, and I knew that. Many foster kids are uniquely denied that type of relationship. Secure home relationships act as a base for all other relationships. I never wanted to disappoint my dad, so my behaviors never got too extreme. Additionally, the fact that I had many solid relationships put me in a position where I did not need to accept a relationship that was abusive or inappropriate. When talking about foster kids, that last point carries a great deal of weight. Since foster kids don't experience secure, unconditional base relationships, they can become very promiscuous and needy, seeking unhealthy relationships, in order to fulfill the desire to feel loved.

We were open for about four months when we brought Tray in. His case manager glossed over some of the pretty serious statements that were made about him in his paperwork when we were interviewing him. Tray was interested in a change of scenery after twenty-two placements, so this fifteen-year-old kid with a 150 IQ told us exactly what we wanted to hear about his past, and we took him in. We quickly learned that Tray had a substance abuse issue, and he was very clever about getting himself high. When off campus, he would buy over-the-counter cold medicine and take dozens of pills at a time. When we got wise to him, he would convince other kids to bring meds in for him. He would make prison wine out of fermented orange peels. One time, he and another kid went into the neighbor's cow pasture and picked what they thought were psilocybin mushrooms off the cow dung and ate them. Within an hour they were doubled over with gastrointestinal pain and transported to the hospital by ambulance. I carried pictures into the emergency room to show them that the mushrooms they ate have been known to cause kidney failure, and the doctor reiterated they would be lucky not to end up on dialysis for the rest of their lives.

I remember a time when we had Tray locked down pretty tight, and I had twenty-five brand-new case managers come for a tour; Tray got up on our fire pit and shouted to them, "Get me the f@#$ out of here," over and over until he was hoarse. At the point when he defecated in a Tupperware box so that he could "huff" the fumes to get high, we realized he needed a serious drug-treatment program if he was going to remain alive. We had him transferred to a higher level of care.

Relating this back to Maslow's Hierarchy of Needs, Tray wasn't embarrassing himself with any of those actions, because he didn't have anybody to be embarrassed in front of. With so many foster placements in such a young life, he didn't truly know anyone on the planet. His actions were completely self-serving, like the actions of a two-year-old. I wish that I could tell you we were able to get him turned around, but we had to move him out for his own safety and the safety of the other kids, as he was influencing them to be drug seeking. Tray should have never been recommended to us and needed serious treatment for his traumatic upbringing and substance abuse. My fear for him is that he will hit rock bottom—usually where most addicts find themselves at the beginning of recovery—because he has no one to recover for. I just pray for him that he will seek God.

Many people have toured our campus since we have opened—approximately a thousand visitors at the date of this writing. A few people have commented that some of the boys' hygiene is not good and that they should do a better job of keeping their rooms clean. One woman who came for a tour, when I was not there to give it myself, sent me a two-page handwritten letter stating that when she raised her boys, they were not allowed free time until their chores were done and their clothes and rooms were clean, and asking why we didn't adopt a similar policy. I admit, initially I was slightly unnerved but managed to smile thinking about the frustration that this woman would have if she were to work with our boys. I wrote her a one-page letter back explaining what I am about to lay out for you in this book. She wrote me back a half-page letter basically saying, "Oh, I didn't know!"

Once we make it into the "Love and Belonging," or "Social," rung of Maslow's hierarchy, we will begin to desire "Esteem" needs. Displaying good hygiene and a clean room, seeking praise for a job well done, and working on our education are a few things that fall into that category. Before we have relationships, however, none of that matters to us. As demonstrated in the story of Tray, there are no negative social consequences for our actions because without relationships, we aren't social! As a side note, when I first saw the Casey Foundation statistic that roughly 80 percent of the adults in the corrections system have been in foster care, I was taken aback, until I realized that only an antisocial person would commit an antisocial act, like stealing someone's property—makes sense.

We have found that getting kids to do their chores, work on their schoolwork, and improve their social behavior can only be accomplished once there is a relationship between the kid and the staff, or at least one staff member. Before that happens, there is nothing we can take away or give to them that will consistently change their behavior.

Prior to starting this foster home, I worked in the juvenile justice field for almost twenty years. We used behavior modification (similar to Pavlov's operant conditioning) with our boys pretty successfully. The difference, however, is that we controlled the one thing those kids really wanted: going home.

Such is a similar control you have as a parent by telling your kid he is grounded and can't spend time with his friends until his behavior changes. As a result, the kid usually changes his behavior. In the juvenile justice programs, I had noticed that when we got a foster kid once or twice a year, they motivated much differently. Boy was I in for wake-up call!

When working with kids where we largely have no control over anything they want, the behavior plan changes significantly. At Crossroads, that looks a lot more like negotiation than punishment.

Assuming you grew up with at least one parent, lived in fewer than three neighborhoods, and went to the same local school throughout your academic career, it is safe to say you have lots of long-term relationships you can reflect on. This reality helps ground you and keeps you from violating any social norms, which might cause you to lose relationships. You understood this even as a kid, and for this reason you didn't consider *only* yourself when committing certain behaviors. You simultaneously considered the judgment of those you had relationships with and people who might influence them regarding their opinion of you.

My foster kids do not have that level of self-accountability. There are no consequences, social or otherwise, to force them into keeping their hygiene up, make them maintain their grades, prevent them from Baker-Acting themselves, or keep them from throwing a tantrum in a public area. Those fences only come with having valuable long-term relationships, and relationships take time. There is no shortcut.

Many of the kids at Crossroads come to us with extreme antisocial behaviors. We have noticed it takes about two months before we start to see buy-in from the kids, and then we start to see meaningful growth after kids have been with us for about five months. We believe that change is a result of relationship building by our staff. The biggest tool we possess to grow those relationships is our remote location, something I will discuss further in chapter 9.

I'm usually able to convince people (like the lady who wrote me that two-page letter) that no one grows financially, educationally, vocationally, or socially (obviously) without having solid relationships. I would also wager, to the degree your relationships are strong, so is your success in any other area. Therein lies the justification for the negative statistics of all foster kids: one in four boys in foster care end up homeless by the age of twenty-two, one in five end up incarcerated, less than 2 percent of foster kids go to college, less than 50 percent get their high school diploma on time at the age of eighteen.

There are a great many different styles of parenting, evidenced by the sheer volume of parenting books out today. Type "parenting books" in any internet search engine and you will get over forty thousand options! Most of them have this one presupposition in common, however: the relationship between the parent and child is valued by both. Removing privileges as a result of bad behavior gets compliance ultimately because the relationship is valued. How often did your teenager run away from home because you took his gaming system away? Foster kids do it all the time. Honestly, although I've used this parenting tactic myself, I have to say, on the surface it is lazy and uncreative.

All behavior, whether it is skipping school or screaming obscenities, has a payoff for the child; otherwise, the behavior would not occur. You are reading this book (behavior) for probably one of three reasons (payoff): you are struggling in your own parenting and are looking for help, you are considering fostering and are gathering info, or you know Crossroads personally and are curious about what I wrote!

When we counsel our kids at Crossroads, we are looking to understand why they behave the way they do. What is the payoff? We ask questions like "When you screamed at the teacher, what were you hoping would happen?" or "What is it that you don't like about school so much that you want to skip all the time?" They are not punitive questions but inquisitive attempts to understand why the kids do what they do. Our purpose for asking is to help problem-solve. We start with the presupposition that all people genuinely want to be successful. No one sets out to be bankrupt, uneducated, and socially inept.

The questions are not asked at the heat of the moment, though, for we all know, when our behavior is emotionally charged, no rational thought processes are happening. Steven Covey said, "Seek first to understand, then to be understood." It is with that mentality we begin asking questions when the time is right.

When Crossroads was a juvenile justice program, our primary method of behavior change was through predictable rewards and consequences. By and large, we had great results with most kids. But again, those kids wanted something we controlled: when they went home. Since we held the key to the one thing they desperately wanted, it was relatively easy to get compliance. Additionally, the vast majority of those kids had relationships. Foster care is a completely different story. Most of our kids are never going home, and they feel so unwanted that they lose their will to care. And let me tell you, that problem is not easily solved with a pep talk.

SECTION II

Humble Beginnings

Chapter 3

Faith over Fear

Jamal

We use relationship building as the structure to change behavior. When a new kid comes in and he is as wild as a feral cat, we spend more time counseling each other than counseling the kid. After Jamal had been two weeks with us, many of the staff wanted to move him out. They said he was destroying our culture, breaking property, undermining staff authority with other kids, and generally a bad fit.

A few staff members, however, saw some positive attributes and had already seen some change. They said Jamal was kind and polite when with him one on one and he would help out when asked. I noticed he was an exceptionally good thank-you card writer (he came to Crossroads right before his birthday). Additionally, our director of operations, Bo, had discovered that Jamal was having a difficult time sleeping at night in his single room. Bo looked back through his file and discovered he was traumatized by his mother who used to lock him in his room when he was small. Clearly this was a contributing factor to his inability to sleep at night.

We moved him to a room with other kids in it and decided collectively to give him a few weeks before making any decisions about kicking him out of the program. In the meantime, all staff began to focus on the few positive things some had noticed. By the end of the month, Jamal was not even visibly the same kid as he had been when he arrived. He was funny and engaging and his kindhearted side really began to show through.

If you look up the word *fear* in the dictionary, you will find the antonym of that word is faith. According to Hebrews 11:1 (NKJV), "Faith is the substance of things hoped for, the evidence of things not seen." I will witness to you that it took a great deal of faith for our board and staff to commit to starting an endeavor that appeared never to have been done before, at least not in Florida.

On May 1, 2012, I received a call from the Florida Department of Juvenile Justice that after twenty-six years as a juvenile residential facility for boys, they would not be renewing our contract as of June 30. The language in the contract gave us only sixty days' notice, meaning I would have to move thirty-five boys to other facilities, give pink slips to thirty employees, and lock the doors of the facility. The recession caused by the housing bubble was taking its toll on everyone, and it appeared imminent that it would soon be the end of an era for Crossroads.

On May 3, our board of directors assembled for an emergency meeting. We had been meeting quarterly for two decades, and the members of the board were notoriously difficult to coordinate schedules with. This was a crisis, however, and everyone was in attendance.

When I was hired by the board back in 2010 to move my family four hours south from Gainesville, I was aware of their reputation. This board did business on *their* terms. Crossroads was fiscally sound and had amassed almost a million dollars in reserves through smart and conservative business practices. The long-term plan was to open a second juvenile justice facility for girls.

The board chair was well known in Charlotte County, and each of the other board members were highly influential in the community. We thought since our corner of the state had a major part in getting then Governor Rick Scott elected, we might survive the impending closure. On this May

Day, however, these established business people and consummate tacticians looked like deer in headlights! "What are we going to do?" The question was directed to me.

"I think I have a plan," I stated.

For almost a year God had intersected me with the foster care system. In June 2011, one of my fellow executive directors seemed to see the writing on the wall and was looking at other options for his juvenile program in south Florida.

"The foster care system has a major problem finding placements for troubled teen boys, and the business model works," he told me. I listened but was not interested. I was working on our own big plans for expansion.

At the time, I was enrolled at the University of South Florida to obtain my board-certified behavior analyst (BCBA) certification. In October of 2011 I was appointed a clinical advisor. During our first phone conversation she asked me, "Is there anything in particular you would like to work on?" I told her that about once or twice a year we would get a foster kid in our juvenile justice program and they did not seem to operate behaviorally or motivationally like other kids. She laughed and told me she had five of her own adopted foster kids. *God knew what He was doing!*

In March of 2012, two months before I would get the fateful call that we were closing, I was sitting in a well-attended juvenile justice council meeting. I had been the secretary of the council for two years. A regional director for foster care happened in, and when given the opportunity, she explained they were having more and more teens with behavioral difficulty coming into the foster care system.

They weren't bad enough for juvenile justice rehabilitation, but no one would take them into their foster homes. She went on to ask if we had any suggestions. I was shocked when the general response of the council was, "Sorry, not our problem." I felt sympathy for her, but more than that, I wondered why I was having so many intersections with the foster care system. Up until that year, I'd never had *any* contact with foster care.

On May 2, I called my executive director friend and asked him to remind me about the details used in the home model for difficult-to-place teen foster boys.

During our May 3rd board meeting, we decided to divide our focus. Half of the board would use their contacts to petition the governor to revisit our contract dissolution, and the other half would begin developing a plan to move forward with foster care.

At the same time, I happened to be in Leadership Charlotte, a yearlong informational program for leaders throughout the community sponsored by the Charlotte County Chamber of Commerce. Being May, we were almost at our graduation date. When I told my class what was happening at Crossroads, they mobilized into action. Almost every leadership class since 1996 had visited Crossroads throughout their year, which had served to cement our facility as a fixture in Charlotte County.

When my class leaders organized a town hall meeting with multiple elected officials speaking, it was no surprise to us that over five hundred people showed up to save our juvenile corrections facility. While most communities scream, "Not in my backyard!" with regard to these kinds of facilities, Charlotte County was taking care of its own.

We were hoping the governor would show up, or at least chime in. That didn't happen, but as a result of the town hall meeting and the 2,500 people who signed a petition on our behalf, Governor Scott gave us two more months to find a solution. Unheard of!

Our outcry and media attention made the secretary of juvenile justice so mad that she picked up her cell phone and dialed mine. When I answered, I said, "Ma'am, I believe you want to talk to my board, I am paid staff." She told me she was intentionally calling me and wanted to know, in essence, why we wouldn't just roll over. I explained our cost of care was a third of the state's cost on their own facilities and our recidivism (long-term success) rates were exceedingly better than theirs with the same population. Not surprisingly, she didn't appreciate my pointing out that fact.

Finally, I shared with her that in March, just two months earlier, the legislature had passed a bill stating although beds needed to be reduced in the juvenile justice world, the state needed to begin by cutting their own beds before cutting private providers, like Crossroads. The secretary chimed in that the bill didn't take effect until July 1 (the beginning of the State's fiscal year), and our contract was up on June 30. I replied, "That's convenient." She repeated matter-of-factly, "It *is* convenient." I was not happy but remained undeterred in my mission to save Crossroads.

Our last juvenile justice kid left on August 31, 2012. Thanks to the kindness of the governor, none of those kids had to be transferred to other facilities to start their time over. They were all able to complete their court-ordered sanctions with us. We got busy immediately retrofitting the facility from bunkhouses to bedrooms and removing everything that screamed "institution" so we could have a home for our new foster population.

My board decided to hire an architect whom I argued with constantly. I told him I didn't want sheetrock in the living spaces, and we needed impact windows. I had worked with boys for the better part of my adult life, and I knew that anger was most satisfactorily taken out on windows and drywall. The architect didn't listen to me, however. Consequently, at the date of this writing we have replaced all the windows in our dorms (nineteen total) more than once. My vocational class got so good at repairing drywall that we considered hiring them out!

Thankfully the local Rotary Foundation gave us a grant and installed impact windows in the dorms. Unfortunately, about half of them have also been replaced. The window manufacturer representative came for a tour and said he had never seen anyone break impact windows with their fists before!

About mid-October of 2012, the disassembly of the bunkhouses was complete and the only thing visible on the two foundations was a frame holding up a roof. The walls, wiring, insulation, and air conditioning ducts had all been removed, and now it was time for reassembly into bedrooms.

I vividly recall one afternoon standing in the middle of construction and feeling a wave of responsibility come over me for charting this course into the unknown. What if we were unable to make this new endeavor work?

What if the expenditure was for naught and forever wasted? My board had wanted to let staff go and keep a skeleton crew while we were going through our renovations since we didn't have any contractual money coming in. I put up a fight by saying it would be impossible to train all new staff for what we were about to experience at a total cost of over half million dollars. What if?

About the time I was having a full-on panic attack, our vocational instructor came up to me and put his arm on my shoulder. "It's not your mission, boss, it's God's!" Enough said. Sanity restored. Momentarily, anyway. As it turns out, most of my staff from the juvenile justice days couldn't make the transition into parenting kids with no self-discipline. Within a year, we had replaced all of them. Live and learn.

While we were without kids in the time period between closing as a DJJ facility and opening as a foster home and school, I sent my two mental health counselors around the state to meet with seventeen different group homes to look at the good and the bad attributes of the business. They learned a lot, and they wrote a forty-page summary of their findings.

When they returned, they both told me I needed to call a guy in Boca Raton who was closing his group home. So I did. When I asked him why they were closing, he told me after twenty years, he was tired. Two weeks prior, the sheriff had shown up in the morning and arrested four kids for "car hopping" (stealing cars to joy ride and then ditching them). He said it was one of a hundred incidents neither he nor his board could stomach anymore. To this day, his words haunt me every time I'm dealing with issues equally as disheartening and frustrating. In my case, however, I believe God called me to do this. If I walked away from this mission, it would be the same as walking away from my faith.

And so, forward we go.

When we wrote our business plan, our fears were not about whether we could turn around the lives of poorly behaved foster boys we were given to steward; we had been turning the lives of young men around for decades. Our concerns were only about the business aspect. Wow were our concerns seriously misplaced! Don't misunderstand me, the financials were often challenging, but what we thought we knew about raising foster boys proved radically wrong.

When we first opened as a foster home and charter school for boys from multiple failed placements, we questioned everything we did with our programming. For the entire first year at Crossroads, I repeatedly wrote in my journal that I feared all we were doing was babysitting. It seemed we were making little or no gain with our boys' behaviors, and the extremity of the behaviors was embarrassing for us to be associated with in our small, tight-knit community.

There's nothing like questioning your actions when the behaviors of the people you care for do not noticeably improve, at least to your expectations. For some reason, however, we stuck with it, and a few years down the road we could see our successes, which served to give us confidence.

Not long after opening, we were getting phone calls from case managers and foster placement specialists who were praising us and saying things like, "Nobody has ever been able to work with that kid before," or "No one has kept him that long before." Often, we had only had them with us for a few weeks! We knew we were onto something based upon these testimonials, and it gave us encouragement despite our own feelings of failure. We just could not wrap our minds around the *why* of the effectiveness of our systems and behavior strategies.

In my mind, it was clear God had opened the doors and made provisions for us to pursue this worthwhile endeavor. I'm confident many of our staff did not see the trees through the forest at first! To say the first six months were difficult would be a gross understatement. In fact, by the six-month mark I had moments where I had been ready to close Crossroads myself to avoid further embarrassment. The fallout from the negative behaviors we were having seemed to have no end.

We stuck it out, though, and at the eight-month mark we began to see that all-important student culture beginning to form. Kids were starting to respect the authority of staff and recognize the value of each other. In some ways they began to work together to achieve common goals. We began to see the light on the horizon.

Chapter 4

Order into Chaos

Arthur

Arthur was one of the first kids we ever took in at Crossroads. I met him and his case manager in our parking lot when he was unpacking his things from the car. He struck me as a sullen and reserved fifteen-year-old, as his responses to my attempts at conversation were brief and strained. As Arthur was pulling a guitar from the trunk of his transporter's car, I mentioned that I played guitar and had just spent $3,500 on one, the most I had ever spent on a guitar. Arthur told me that he had a $20,000 guitar, but his last foster mother was keeping it for him. That "story" would prove to be the first of many fantastic tales from our foster boys I would be witness to through the years. Sure, kids and teens can tend to bend the truth; it's part of growing up. However, the tales our boys were telling were so far out of the realm of possibility that no one could believe them. We had a lot to learn.

After four months of renovations, the new facility was finished. It was beautiful! We had our grand opening and blessing of the facilities on December 2, 2012. Over two hundred people drove the twenty miles out to our remote location to be part of the celebration.

We moved our first foster boy into the program on Thursday, January 3, 2013. Arthur and another kid came in the next day. The staff nervously anticipated their arrivals with a mixture of excitement and apprehension, as we had no idea what we were getting into.

Having five teachers and three kids those first few days was a bit odd, but the kids loved the attention. By the end of January, we had nine kids. The new problem we had was balancing how quickly we could bring these volatile foster boys in while at the same time worrying about going bankrupt. We had budgeted on having nineteen kids every day and were bleeding money profusely. It actually took us until June before we hit that number, and by then we were in debt $120,000. My board wanted to strangle me!

My team leader called me on a Sunday morning late in January. She told me one of the boys had written in indelible marker on his bedroom wall—our brand-new walls. I could feel my blood pressure rise. In the DJJ days, I would walk through the dorms every morning, and if there was even a hint of graffiti in the bathroom or bunk beds, the entire dorm would use the bathroom in the woods for a week. Actions like that put pressure on the kids who were close to graduation to keep the new kids in line in the DJJ world.

My team leader texted me a picture of what was written. It said, "This is my room." I instantly felt remorseful. In true military fashion, I had always told my DJJ kids, "This is my house. You will respect it." But this was different. Those DJJ kids were working to get home; they were visitors. These kids *were* home. And for so many of them, having come from circumstances and living conditions that no human should have to call home, a space of their own had been a distant dream.

I contacted some resources, and when I came in on Monday, I brought posters and framed pictures for the kids to choose from. I asked them not to write on their walls and told them I would provide them with pictures of their choice if they wanted to decorate their rooms. Although I thought I understood the problem at this point, I still had so much to learn.

The phone calls I was getting at night from the team leaders were insane. Kids were fighting, running through the woods, destroying stuff, breaking into other buildings, stealing from each other, and regularly invoking the Baker Act, which means they get locked inside a mental health facility voluntarily for seventy-two hours.

The sheriff called me to a meeting in June and showed me a report. In 2010 Crossroads had one call to the sheriff's office. In 2011 we had three. In 2012 we had none. In the first six months of 2013 as a foster home, we already had 160 calls!

I assured the sheriff that it took time to develop a student culture and we were getting closer. In reality, though, I was wondering if what we were doing was even possible. I was tired of the behavior and destruction. I had worked at thirteen DJJ facilities in my career and was always able to get a stable student culture by six months. I admit I almost pulled the plug at this point. Would we ever get over our growing pains?

By August, however, we started seeing the semblance of a culture developing. Kids were accepting consequences for their behavior; more than half of the boys had been with me for six months or more, so their behavior triggers weren't as sensitive. We started having hope this experiment could work.

I say "experiment" because during the time right before opening, when we had no kids, I looked across the country to see if there was an example we could position ourselves after. There didn't seem to be any. We truly were blazing new trails. Almost all foster homes were within communities versus in remote locations, and no other placement in Florida had a charter school on site. Their kids all attended public schools.

In contrast, Crossroads is twenty miles from the nearest gas station and our nearest neighbor is three miles down the road. Before we opened, I had several critics, one being a local business woman who had been in the foster care system as a child. She told me it wasn't right to raise foster boys in the middle of nowhere. She was adamant they should have the opportunity to attend regular school and not be "kept out in the woods."

Now, after eight years of taking behaviorally difficult boys who are prone to running away and who have not attended school on average for two years, I'm so thankful I didn't embrace that mind-set. As it turns out, being in a remote setting has had distinct advantages.

SECTION III

The Nitty Gritty

Chapter 5

How Do You Get Your Kids?

Jonathan

Jonathan told our director of operations everything he wanted to hear during his phone interview. When Jonathan arrived on campus with his caseworker, he was pleasant and respectful and seemed genuinely excited to be at Crossroads. When his caseworker drove out of the parking lot and was out of eyesight, however, Jonathan began to curse at all of us, then walked outside to sit at a picnic table. At that moment, all the kids and staff were heading to the cafeteria for an afternoon snack and shift change. I looked out my window and saw our director of education walk up to greet him. She peeled off quickly, however; clearly, he wasn't being friendly.

I walked out of my office and headed to greet Jonathan. We hadn't met yet; I only heard a little of his personality from down the hallway. He immediately began threatening and cursing me. After a few quiet moments, he offered that he wasn't staying; he was just "messing" with his caseworker who had just driven him the two hours to get to Crossroads. We had no choice but to call her and have her come pick him up. She looked frustrated when she got there but seemed to know Jonathan's games all too well.

When I am asked how kids become enrolled at Crossroads, I take for granted the foster care system is foreign to most people. We receive calls

35

daily (about two to three) from placing agencies around the state who are having difficulty placing their teen boys with foster homes. They email us the youth's psychological evaluations, educational materials, behavior reports, legal documents, and any other information about the youth that they have.

Our case manager, our director of education, and our director of operations look over the information and decide whether to interview the potential placement. We like to do the interview in person, but for practicality, we conduct most of them over the phone or video conference.

Our staff talk directly to the youth about any questions they have from what was reviewed in their paperwork. This can be interesting because 90 percent of the time the youth's case manager wants to answer for him, and we have to remind the case manager the interview is with the youth and not them.

Quite frequently, case managers will gloss over areas of major concern with a child in their effort to place him. There is always a shortage of appropriate placements for foster kids, and it is common for kids to sleep supervised in hotels or even in case manager's offices until they can be placed. Recently a placing agency called to find out if we had any open beds because they had thirteen teens with them in their offices awaiting placement. I suspect that supervising kids after hours plays a big role in job burnout for case managers in the foster care system.

Once all the questions are answered about any concerns, our director of operations (DO) lets the youth know the expectations we have at Crossroads for each kid. Some of what we expect from our residents include the following:

- Helping out with chores

- Being respectful to staff and other kids

- Expressing themselves appropriately

- Showing up for counseling appointments

- Accepting consequences for inappropriate behavior or breaking rules

- Attending school

In addition, the DO lets them know they most likely will be going to school on-site, there are no girls on our campus, and we are twenty miles from town. The decision is then left up to the kid if he wants to come. Any of those things may be a deal breaker, but in most cases they don't have other options and they end up coming to us.

When we are looking at their paperwork, we exclude kids who have a lower-than-normal IQ, might be a danger to other kids, are not ambulatory, or have extreme allergies. Our education department is small, and unfortunately, we are not able to handle extreme learning difficulties. Also, it takes the ambulance about thirty minutes to reach us, so if a kid has a serious medical issue, it could be detrimental to his health to come to Crossroads.

Most of the boys who come to Crossroads are happy about their decision. The ones who have instant regrets are usually the ones who come from the bigger cities in Florida. They have never been in the woods before. The lack of city noise and lights and the smell of country air can be unsettling to them. Over time, however, the vast majority of kids come to appreciate the lack of distractions. Most importantly, they develop relationships with staff members, which helps them feel connected to something. By now, we have about one kid per month who has left us unfavorably for some reason but now wants to come back to Crossroads.

In the state of Florida, foster care is largely privatized. The Department of Children and Families (DCF) subcontracts with seventeen nonprofit Community-Based Care (CBC) organizations around the state. These organizations are responsible for the care, placement, and follow-up of the state's foster kids. It is an exceptionally good system. Some of you may think the government should have sole control over such a delicate population, but I'd like to suggest otherwise based upon years of experience.

Philosophically, all government agencies operate under two primary focuses: cost and liability. In the human service field and, in this case, foster care, those focuses are diametrically opposed to what is best for the individual: the foster child.

Until 2013, Florida had a law on the books that said if a foster child was spending the night away from their foster home, the visiting home had to have a home study completed with everyone in the household having completed background checks. Did you get background checks done on your son's friends' families before he went to spend the night with them? Of course not; you used prudent parenting techniques to ensure his safety. Fortunately, our legislature eventually agreed with normalcy and prudent parenting, and those laws were changed.

Government agencies will always err on the side of caution for liability reasons. By contrast, a nonprofit organization is focused (ideally) on the mission. At Crossroads we always look to do what's best for each individual youth.

For example, I don't budget for our kids to play high school or recreation league sports because so many of them don't. If the government agency is in charge, written permission from the legal guardian or court official is required for them to play in the first place, and then there is the red tape to go through to pay for the expenditure. Anyone with any experience with a government entity and budget knows this isn't an easy task; the tape couldn't get any more red.

In the nonprofit world, however, when I have a kid who wants to participate in extracurricular activities, our team can evaluate the situation and work out the details of transportation, timing, etc. Then I can ask my donor base to sponsor them for any related expenses. Gratefully, someone always does. Our donors are incredibly supportive, and we couldn't do what we do without their constant and unwavering support and generosity.

Most of our kids either age out with us or we have them removed because they become a danger to themselves or other kids. Occasionally, however, a case manager, a guardian ad litem, or family court judge will remove a boy from Crossroads. We are rarely in agreement with them, which is frustrating. A few of our kids, very few, are reunited with family members.

A few years ago one of our sixteen-year-old kids, a boy named Carl, had a family court hearing by telephone. My case manager, director of education, and mental health counselor were on the phone along with him at Crossroads. One the other end of the line in Gainesville was his guardian ad litem, case manager, and lawyer ad litem along with the family court judge.

The judge told Carl he had contacted his grandfather in Illinois, who had gotten out of prison and would now like Carl to come and live with him. Carl told everyone on the call that he had not seen his grandfather since he was nine years old and didn't even know him. Additionally, he told the judge he was doing well at Crossroads and finally felt like he belonged somewhere and didn't want to leave. The case manager in Gainesville reiterated that fact to the judge. However, the judge told Carl his mind was made up and he would be leaving by the end of the week to go to Illinois. Carl burst into tears, and when I heard about the whole story, I was angry.

I made an appointment with the judge and magistrate. Two weeks later I drove four hours up to Gainesville to meet with them. I asked them to look me in the eye and tell me they would have made the same decision if their own son was in that situation. They blubbered something about the law, and I gave them three examples from around the state of similar situations with Crossroads kids that weren't handled the way their court just handled it. They didn't relent or apologize, but I suspect that to this day they haven't forgotten me, and since then that court has not messed with any of our kids—a small consolation. I still wonder about Carl, though, and hope he is doing all right.

On another occasion, the guardian ad litem for one of our kids told his family court judge that it was too difficult for her to drive three hours across the state to visit her court-appointed youth at Crossroads. The kid's case manager tried to explain to the judge there were no closer placements that would accept him and the thirteen-year-old was currently doing the best he had ever done anywhere. The judge didn't want to hear it and gave the case manager thirty days to move him back to their county. On the thirtieth day there were no placements for Tommy, so they moved him to a runaway shelter in their community. Chaos!

The foster care system is far from perfect. Difficult decisions can have dire consequences in the life of a child. We have gotten much better over the years at screening the kids we bring into our home, for everyone's safety. But once they come to us, we treat them like they are our own and fight whatever battles we need to fight in order to ensure their success.

Chapter 6

Removal from Home—Entering Foster Care

Michael

B oth Michael's biological parents were dead. The fifteen-year-old came to us from a foster family who would punish him and his brother by locking them in a closet and forcing them to beat one another. If one would get in trouble, they would force the other brother to beat him to their satisfaction. If they weren't satisfied, the foster parents would beat both kids. Needless to say, the kids were removed, and the foster parents went to jail. The brothers were sent to another foster home, but Michael began to have behavior issues the family couldn't handle, so he was sent to Crossroads.

You may be interested in the reasons why kids are removed from their homes and placed in foster care. If you were to talk to some of the families who have had their kids taken away, you might get a bad taste in your mouth for Child Protective Services. However, as a practitioner, I can assure you the initial removal of the kid from his home is almost always justified. At least that has been my experience in the state of Florida.

Child Protective Services takes their job very seriously. In fact, from what I have read in the kids' case files as we intake the youths in our charge, they probably should have been removed far sooner than they originally were. After the kid is removed, though, lines get blurred and things can get messy.

When a child is removed from their home in Florida, the parents receive a trained mediator from the family court. They are usually given a set of conditions they must meet in order to get their children back. Attending drug counseling, getting and keeping a job, and keeping the house picked up and sanitary are just a few of those conditions, which could include many others depending upon the situation.

What we have seen in the cases of our Crossroads kids is that their parents either ignore the court or lose their struggle with addiction. Either way they cannot keep up with the expectations of the court. At some point, in many cases (and this varies from circuit to circuit), the parents' rights are terminated, and the kids become true wards of the state.

Here are the top ten reasons why children are removed from their homes, according to the 2020 U. S. Department of Health and Human Services, specifically the Adoption and Foster Care Analysis and Reporting System (AFCARS):

- 62 percent – Neglect

- 36 percent – Drug abuse

- 14 percent – Caregiver unable to cope

- 12 percent – Physical abuse

- 10 percent – Lack of adequate housing

- 9 percent – Child behavior problem

- 7 percent – Parental incarceration

- 5 percent – Parental alcohol abuse

- 5 percent – Abandonment

- 4 percent – Sexual abuse[1]

At Crossroads we tend to see some of the more extreme cases of removal. Usually, kids are not new to the foster care system when they come to us. I would estimate, about 10 percent of the time our kids have a parent or family member who is trying to get them back. In most of those cases, the caregivers struggle with understanding or complying with family court sanctions.

It is agonizing for us to watch our kids struggle to understand why their parent won't pass a drug test to get them back. As you might well imagine, feelings of not being worth fighting for, feeling inadequate, or blaming themselves are common. Worse yet are the scenarios where a parent has a terminal illness and is physically incapable or unable to care for their child. Some of our angriest boys have had to endure that unfortunate situation.

Very rarely have I seen a kid who did not want to go back to their parents—regardless of how heinous the abuse was to them in the home. Proverbs 17:6 says, "The glory of children is their fathers." We have seen that to be true. The reality for us, though, is that only about 10 percent of our kids ever get reunited with their families.

I remember one boy whose father had been to jail for the violence against him and his mother. Both parents lost their parental rights because of the violence in the home. And yet, our kid just wanted to go home. The parents would drive three hours across the state just to post love notes to him on the telephone poles down our dirt road. It spooked some of my staff members who knew the history of the family.

---

[1]   U. S. Department of Health and Human Services, "The AFCARS Report," accessed March 11, 2022, https://www.acf.hhs.gov/sites/default/files/documents/cb/afcarsreport28.pdf.

I ended up calling the father's parole officer, as he wasn't supposed to be out of his county, let alone visiting his son. It was pointless to talk to the kid about his father, though. He defended his actions fiercely (again, see Proverbs 17:6).

When the Department of Children and Families (DCF) gets involved with a family, their number one goal is to make sure that everyone in the household is safe. Second to that, they want to keep it that way and place a high priority on keeping the family together. It is only in extreme situations where the DCF child protective services petitions to remove the kids from their homes.

Child protective services workers have an unenviable job with high burn-out rates and I'm certain they incur Post Traumatic Stress Disorder (PTSD) from their jobs. Unfortunately, they are necessary to protect our most vulnerable population. Removing kids from the home isn't ultimately their decision, it is the courts, but they are the first line of defense for kids.

Chapter 7

Turning Eighteen

Adam

Adam was turning eighteen in two months and was excited about being free from foster care. He had been with us for almost two years, and although he had made some gains in his education, he was still only registered as a freshman. We convinced him to work toward his GED, but as he got closer to aging out of foster care, he cared less about studying. I and other staff had many motivational discussions with him to get him back in the classroom over the time he was with us.

One morning I looked out and Adam was wandering around campus with no shirt or shoes on and a cowboy hat on his head. I yelled out the window, "Why aren't you in school?" Adam replied, "I'll do that after I leave here." I walked out and tried to explain to him that there is no switch that goes off making you responsible, that you have to practice responsibility to get better at it, and you have to have responsibility to achieve anything.

Upon leaving Crossroads, we had Adam set up to work on his GED at nights in the mall close to where he was living. About a month after he left Crossroads, he called me at supper time and asked me to come and get him from the mall. I said, "I thought your GED program went to seven p.m. and it's only 5:45." He said, "I don't like the teacher and I'm leaving." I told him to stay where he was, and I would pick him up and take him to dinner.

I know the people sitting around us in the restaurant thought I was being pretty tough on him—I could see it in their glances toward our table—but Adam didn't have a lot of options if he didn't stick to the plan. My counsel didn't last long, though, because within a month he refused to keep working on his GED. Shortly after, he lost the entitlement money he was using to pay rent and became homeless.

A frequent question I get when speaking with different organizations is, "What happens to a kid when he turns eighteen?" The answer is complicated. As soon as we started taking in foster kids, we began to realize we were going to need a support system for them once they turned eighteen.

We started a second nonprofit organization called Crossroads Transitions, formed a board, and at one time had a part-time staff member. We partnered with the local homeless coalition who let us use a house, which had been donated to them, for four of our eighteen-year-olds. Our board members would interview kids wanting to live there and then, once they moved in, checked up on them periodically to make sure they had everything they needed. The part-time staff member was hired to cover the gap, as we noticed the kids needed more attention than we originally anticipated. After some time, we just realized it was like an perpetual "spring break" at the house. We really tried to make that endeavor work, but after two years we mothballed the transition house for many of the reasons I'll talk about next.

Very few foster kids who turn eighteen are ready to be on their own. Kids who come from a somewhat normal family typically have a support system after they move out. Our Crossroads kids for the most part only have us. I don't know about you, but I called my mom every week after I left home. Through college, military service, and even into marriage. Sometimes it was just to find out how to make a chicken salad sandwich (pre-Google)! The point is that anyone who is successful or has self-discipline should thank their support network. Without relationships, neither of those things is likely.

Foster kids don't have accountability systems, for the most part, and once they are legal adults, they can get themselves rapidly into hot water. It is a contributing factor as to why so many foster kids end up homeless or incarcerated as adults.

I would say about 50 percent of our kids do not have their driver's licenses by the time they turn eighteen. Getting their birth certificates can be extremely difficult sometimes too. Taking the four-hour drug and alcohol class (required for permit) and the online permitting class itself is a challenge, especially with kids who are on a low reading level. Then there is the coordination of driver's education, which our school district thankfully pays for. And finally, finding a vehicle to use for the driving portion of the driver's license test. I personally have had four kids take the driver's test in my full-size truck—not ideal for testing. My insurance agent (a Crossroads board member) has since warned me against that practice.

At Crossroads we are thinking about their eighteenth birthday the day the kid comes to us. Once the boy turns seventeen, that process really ramps up. Without having a consistent place to refer them to, like our Crossroads Transitions house, there is currently no universal plan for our kids as they age out.

Since the closing of Transitions, we have been fortunate enough to be able to help each one of our eighteen-year-olds find lodging, school programs, and/or jobs. That has happened sometimes through their own relatives, sometimes through our staff members, and sometimes through our volunteer mentors.

In a recent situation, Nick, while still seventeen, earned his GED (General Education Diploma, similar to a high school diploma) and enrolled in college. Nick completed three semesters of college while he was with us, and during that time he had also grown remarkably close to Dave, one of our volunteers. Dave picked Nick up at Crossroads every Sunday, for months before he turned eighteen, and took him to church, then to his home to enjoy a homecooked meal with his family. As Nick's birthday drew closer, Dave helped him find an apartment and a vehicle. After Nick turned eighteen, Dave continued to mentor him and bring him to the house weekly. Eventually, after completing three years of college, Nick joined the army. Nick and Dave continue to communicate weekly.

Above anything else, Nick will always have Dave and his wife, Teri, to thank for his success after Crossroads. It is likely without that support he would have been a statistic through bad choices and lack of commitment to better his own future. I wish we could find mentors like that for all our boys! I'm confident our success rate would be significantly better if each of them had their own volunteer, a caring adult, to guide them into adulthood.

Fortunately, we have access to resources such as cars and living expenses for our eighteen-and-older population through donors who are more than willing to help. Every situation is different, and as we have more and more boys come through our doors, we also have more and more needs to fill. Sometimes it takes a bit of creativity to make it all come together.

As an example, Randy was doing fine at his college until he realized they were closing the dorms for Christmas break. Randy would have been homeless for two weeks if we hadn't jumped into action. The bigger problem was going to be when they closed the dorms for the summer and he would need alternative living for two months. Fortunately, one of our board members was also on that college's board and was able to get special arrangements made through the housing director, but these are the types of problems most kids going to school don't have to worry about. They go home to their families when school isn't in session. But what do you do if you have a kid without any family to rely on?

Of all the kids who have aged out of foster care with Crossroads, with the exception of those who had mentors, very few have been successful in the short term after leaving. Many foster kids look forward to turning eighteen and being "out of the system," but they are grossly ill prepared for adulthood. They lack the self-discipline to stick to the plan we have worked out with them. Many of our eighteen-year-olds become homeless within a few months of aging out—primarily due to poor choices and behavior. Then we have to help them pick up the pieces.

Very recently I had two former students (separately) call me because they were homeless. I hadn't seen either of them in more than two years. In my estimation, both have burned their bridges and were grasping at straws by calling people with whom they have not maintained relationships. When anyone calls me, former foster kid or not, I will do my best to help them. I will not, however, enable bad behavior.

Three years ago, I had a twenty-one-year-old former Crossroads kid call me. He had been living in a twenty-four-foot boat on a trailer in a storage yard. A few of our volunteers would take him food periodically, but he couldn't keep a job due to drug usage.

I picked him up one morning because he asked to come talk to the staff and kids at Crossroads. Taking him home that afternoon, he explained to me how it was everyone else's fault he couldn't keep a job. When he asked me if I would help him find a place to stay, I told him that I would but only if he first agreed to see a counselor about his drug problem twice a week for a month first. He declined. Eventually, he got it together and now has a job and a child. He still calls from time to time.

I can't overemphasize enough how important relationships are to the success of foster kids. The frustratingly difficult part is trying to find adults who are willing to sacrifice themselves enough to get close to them. What we have learned is that in the best case, a mentor gets to know a kid while he is still in our care, then transitions the relationship once the kid ages out of foster care, like in the story of Dave and Teri with Nick.

What we have noticed is that kids are more willing to spend time with a mentor while they are living at Crossroads, their "home." Once they turn eighteen, they believe themselves to be "grown" and have no desire to hang out with adults even if they are just trying to help them avoid the pitfalls of life.

Years ago I was trying to convince a friend of mine who was also a captain on the local police force to become a mentor. He said to me, "John, I'll come out to the birthday parties and special occasions, but I don't have time right now to be a mentor." At one birthday party he sat down next to a seventeen-year-old named Darryl. He asked, "What do you want to be when you grow up?"

Darryl told him he wanted to be a firefighter, so my friend told him he worked next to the fire station and maybe he could take him for a tour sometime. My friend came and asked me for permission, and of course I agreed to allow it.

The funny thing about Darryl was in the six months I had known him, I never heard him speak once. I thought the half-hour car ride to and from the fire station was going to be miserable for my friend, but when he brought Darryl back to campus, he was almost giddy. He said, "Man, that is a great kid, and we talked about this, and we talked about that."

Over the course of the next six months, my friend was progressively involving Darryl more and more with his family. They were going to the beach, shopping, visiting museums, and eventually spending weekends together at my friend's home. By the time Darryl turned eighteen and got his GED, my friend and his wife considered him a son. They helped him find an apartment and get enrolled in college. My friend had unwittingly become Darryl's mentor!

This is an example of a best-case scenario for a mentorship. Relationships can't be forced; they need to happen organically. On our volunteer information sheet, I have a request for volunteer mentors. When I speak to groups, I usually mention the need for mentors, but often the reason they want to mentor isn't a great fit for our boys. One time after speaking at a big church, a guy made an appointment with me to come out to explore the possibility of mentoring. After talking to him for a while, it became apparent to me that he just wanted to download himself into a kid because he was proud of his varied life experiences. While having interesting life experiences can be personally rewarding, a kid honestly isn't interested in what you've done, and he won't be impressed with your work history. Focusing on the kid and *listening* to him, rather than having a desire to impart your wisdom, is great way to start the relationship. Steven Covey's "seek first to understand" quote is highly relevant when mentoring kids.

I wish I could tell you there is an easy solution for kids aging out of foster care, but there is not. Our culture and laws mandate that an eighteen-year-old is a legal adult. Support services become much more complicated to access for an adult, if they are existent at all. Many of the kids who leave Crossroads are also deluded into believing they are fully adult at eighteen, causing them to make a series of compounding bad decisions.

After six months of being off our radar, they are usually in serious need of help. By the time they contact us, we have many times seen them homeless or worse because they've lost their jobs or refused to comply with extended foster care requirements, thereby losing their funding.

My hope is that one day we will be able to revisit having a dorm-style living facility for our eighteen-and-up population. We've learned, for that to be successful, we will need a full-time chaperone living there, maybe two, preferably retired military. Having someone to be both mentor and disciplinarian would be ideal and what these boys desperately need. I envision someone who is seasoned, a little salty, and able to hold the kids accountable as a perfect fit for that job.

I think it would also be important to have other kids living there who are focused on success, like college kids or young adults in the trades. Having stable, success-minded kids in the same living space would help create a success-minded culture.

Ideally, if we were going to have a "dorm," we would have a concrete building with small studio-like apartments with no family room for gatherings. The idea is that if the place is small enough, there won't be room to invite someone over to hang out or stay. The chaperone living on the property would mentor, push the boys to be responsible, and not allow undesirable behaviors. If the chaperone is able to catch small issues and behaviors early on, those problems would likely not become major ones later. The property should also be near jobs, vocational school, and shopping so that the boys wouldn't have to depend upon personal transportation, which can be another challenge for foster kids.

I should mention before I close this chapter that we have a boyhood to manhood ceremony when a kid turns eighteen at Crossroads; we call it a "Crossing Over." One of our board members recognized that we needed a ceremony when a kid was turning eighteen and leaving Crossroads, in order to close this chapter of his life. It has become a showpiece for us, and even though we may only have two or three per year, we usually have twenty or more volunteers drive out to attend each time. We get our kids sponsored for their Crossing Over, much like birthdays. One of my board members pays for the young man to get a new suit and tie. A volunteer sponsors him for presents that will help him in his newly independent life, too, usually tools or items for his apartment.

The ceremony begins with the boy placing his pre-ordered name plate on the tribal spear, which we feature in our main office, where all the other eighteen-year-olds before him have placed their names. He steps out of the office with a pre-lit torch and walks to the fire pit. Nine of the boys stand in a circle around the fire pit behind an unlit tiki torch. A board member escorts the eighteen-year-old around the circle where he lights a torch, and the boy guarding it recites one of our core values and a passage about being successful. After finishing the circle and lighting all the tiki torches, the board member attendant places a tie and jacket on the young man and introduces him as our newest Crossroads alumnus. At that time the rest of the kids and the staff can make comments to the boy turning eighteen, and he, in turn, will usually give some advice to the younger boys who are watching him leave. There are almost always tears, and more than once we have had a kid who was days from his eighteenth birthday exclaim that he is not ready to leave Crossroads.

SECTION IV

Nuts and Bolts

Chapter 8

Fostering Hope

Antonio

Antonio was working on his driver's permit and had some questions for me. I could smell the sixteen-year-old before he even got to my office. I don't think he had showered in a week, and it looked like he hadn't changed his clothes in the same time frame. I tried to be gentle. "Antonio, is there a reason why you can't take a shower?" He replied, "I haven't had time."

After a discussion about cleanliness and appropriate appearances, especially to be appealing to girls, a discussion I'm sure other staff had had with him, we turned to the issue of the driver's permit. "You know you have to complete the four-hour drug and alcohol course before you can get your permit, right?" He replied," Oh, I'm not going to do hard drugs while I drive. I may drink a little, but I won't be drunk." I wish I could tell you that he was kidding. Our kids have so much to learn, or maybe, unlearn.

--------------------------◆◆◆--------------------------

Stability

There is a ton of research out there demonstrating how important consistency and stability in the home are when raising kids. There are plenty of studies showing that relational instability in the home is detrimental to the upbringing of kids.

It probably seems like common sense that stability is good for kids, especially foster kids, and instability is bad. The laws in many states conflict with that reasoning, however, resulting in foster kids averaging three placements, according to national statistics. In Florida the average is higher, and on average the teens we take at Crossroads have been to fourteen different placements before coming here. We had one kid who had been to sixty-four placements before coming to Crossroads!

Academically, instability stunts learning growth. One study suggested that every time a foster kid changes placement, he goes backward a grade in aptitude. While that may not seem possible for a kid who has been to sixty-four placements, our experience in our charter school is that the basic educational skills of our twelve- to eighteen-year-olds is detrimentally low. Using standardized testing, we've consistently seen the average reading level of our boys to be at fifth grade. In other words, these are the average reading skills of a ten-year-old.

Instability and multiple placements cause foster kids to struggle with making meaningful relationships, sometimes becoming a lifelong issue. Trust takes time to develop and is foundational to relationships. Each time a kid moves from one placement to another, he is putting up more barriers to acceptance of relationships with people around him. His desire for a relationship doesn't decrease, but his ability to believe he will have them decreases.

Statistically speaking, instability of foster kids also negatively impacts the future possibility of permanency of placement. One study demonstrates that 33 percent of foster kids with one placement eventually reunite with their parents. Juxtapose that number with only 13 percent reuniting with parents after their second placement. Less than 5 percent reunite after their third placement. Obviously, there are a lot of variables in that statistic, but I think it adds to the argument that stability should be the number one goal of the entire foster care system.

In Florida, kids are given a voice as to where they will be placed and whether or not they should move placements. That ability to choose is a double-edged sword. On the one hand, allowing the kid a choice can garner buy-in for the move to the new placement. On the other hand, we have seen caseworkers give in to the demands of the child similar to a parent having a moment of weakness with their own child. "I want to leave this place and I want to leave here right now!" Long-term, however, the chances for success decrease for the child with every relocation.

Then there are kids who sabotage their placements through exhibiting intolerable behavior. At Crossroads, if a kid is a danger to other kids, we have no choice but to move him. Sometimes, however, that is exactly what he is looking for. Sometimes we take in a kid who should have never been placed with us. An overworked case manager glosses over certain behaviors or medical problems we are not equipped to handle, and we end up with a kid whose health is seriously compromised by being with us. We have no choice but to move him, and in the end we become just another failed placement for him.

Forgiveness

Jesus said, "For if you forgive others their transpasses, your heavenly Father will forgive you, but if you do not forgive others their trespasses, neither will your Father forgive your trespasses" (Matthew 6:14).

Our American culture has become all about vindication. There are so many movies out that display revenge or glorify vengeful behavior. It is almost unheard of to see someone do what Jesus was talking about. We want justice when someone slights us, cuts us off in traffic, or attacks our character. The social norm is to seek retribution.

What if you are raising a child who lashes out when you are trying to parent them? Even our cultural parenting norm is to punish them when our expectations aren't met, taking away video games, grounding them, or using time-outs. Those strategies are not always effective with every child, and employing them can be damaging to the parent-child relationship. I would like to talk about what forgiveness can look like in the heat of the moment.

One morning at Crossroads, two boys got in a fight in the cafeteria. Staff were able to move the bigger boy outside the cafeteria, but tempers and blood pressures were still high. Our food services manager, Ms. Shelly, stood in the doorway, and although the aggressor was trying to get back into the kitchen to continue the fight, Ms. Shelly stood her ground and verbally praised the kid for respecting her enough not to touch her in his attempt to get inside. Their relationship is stronger now.

Shelly's kitchen received some damage in the fight, and her plan for breakfast was put on hold due to the disruption. There were plenty of things she could have been mad about and wanted justice for, but in the crucial moment, she focused on the kid's one positive behavior: in his anger, he didn't harm her. You may not think Shelly's comments toward the boy constituted forgiveness at the time, but if you look closely, she did not hold the boy's anger against him. What, after all, is forgiveness?

In the heat of the moment, when you are most frustrated with your own child's behavior, you are likely to say or do something you will regret later. Those things usually come from a desire for power and control. If you can acknowledge that desire in the adverse times, you will be less likely to damage the relationship when things are not as they should be. I am not at all suggesting there should not be consequences for unmet expectations; there should be. I am suggesting that setting clear expectations and negotiating behaviors and consequences, both positive and negative, should be done at a time when emotions are not heightened.

In the case of the fight, Matt, the bigger kid, was defending himself. He was not the initiator. Still, fighting is not socially appropriate or responsible behavior, and there were consequences for both boys, which were negotiated with them after they calmed down.

One Monday morning I came on campus and a kid was kicking the front door of the main office and screaming obscenities. Two staff were standing with him on the porch to make sure he didn't get too far out of control, and they were trying to convince him to go to school. As I walked up, I said, "Good morning, Jamie, what's going on?" He replied angrily that the staff weren't treating him right, his room was messed up, he wanted to go back to Tallahassee so he would be closer to his family, and he wanted to go to public school.

I asked Jamie why he didn't bring any of those things up to me on Friday when I talked to him, and he just raised his voice. I kept calm and acknowledged his frustration and, rather than going in the office, walked toward the cafeteria. He followed me. We both went inside, and I began talking with Ms. Shelly about inconsequential things. Ms. Shelly smiled at Jamie and asked him if he wanted to help her, but he wasn't in the mood yet.

For about ten minutes Shelly and I talked about random topics to give Jamie time to calm down. We did not look at him or acknowledge that he was having an issue; we pretended we were in our own little world until we could sense he was calm.

The entire situation with Jamie was about his unwillingness to get out of bed that morning and my staff's frustration with trying to get him up. Once he was out of bed, his unspoken goal was to make sure everyone knew he wasn't happy, and he succeeded. I didn't like the fact he was kicking the door of the office, but if I would have focused on that in the moment, I would have escalated the situation. I let it go (forgave him), brought him to a new environment (the cafeteria) with a new person (Shelly), and gave him time to calm down. I also looked him in the eye, acknowledged him as a person, not a problem to be dealt with, and gave him back the dignity he lost in his temper tantrum from earlier. He ended up going back to school and was fine the rest of the day.

In parenting and in caregiving with children, practicing forgiveness is crucial to building relationally strong people. Look closely at the causes of your child's negative behavior, negotiate change, and *always* forgive when your child disappoints you!

Delayed Gratification

I suppose we could agree that all kids have difficulties waiting for results and working for future outcomes, but my observations are that delayed gratification is much worse with foster kids. As parents we require our kids to wait from an early age. We teach them to sit patiently; we make them wait until we are done speaking and don't allow them to interrupt us. We make them wait until the end of the week for their allowance. We make them sit quietly in church. For our foster boys, especially when they are new to us, it seems they can't wait for anything!

One weekend we had a local family fun park call to ask if we could have kids come and help hand out flyers and direct parking for the weekend. We didn't know how much they were going to pay the kids or when they would settle accounts after the event, so we told the boys as much. On Saturday afternoon I got a call from the park saying the kids kept asking when they would be paid and how much. I assured him we had thoroughly explained to the kids it could be weeks, but it was the nature of our teens to behave that way. The park manager said the kids were putting him in a very uncomfortable situation.

The following weekend, after officially hiring five of the boys, two of them did not go back to work on Sunday after working Saturday because "it was boring." I wish it was the only occurrence like that when we found jobs for kids, but it wasn't. Our boys had a difficult time accepting that they had to wait for their paychecks. I'm sure their previous instability in placements exacerbated their anxiety over waiting to be paid too.

The volunteer who ran our pottery studio had taught at Penn State and was retired from an extensive career in teaching pottery. He was methodical in preparing kids to work with clay but was amazed that very few kids would come back a second day to learn new skills. As far as I know, no kid ever made it all the way to using the pottery wheel, which requires extensive preparation, because they got impatient with the learning process.

We had the same experience in our vocational program. Most of our kids were too impatient to take the time to learn how to use the machines safely in order to progress forward with building bigger and better things. This was something that never occurred when we were working with the juvenile justice kids.

As another argument for stability, I would point out that the kids who did better in the job situations and better in the vocational settings with us were our kids who had been with us for a longer period of time. They also were observably more patient in their communication with staff and other adults, and more appreciative of the volunteers. I can't overemphasize how important stability of placement is to the raising of healthy foster kids.

Empathy

Merriam-Webster defines empathy as "one's ability to recognize, perceive, and feel directly the emotion of another." Empathy can be a difficult thing to recognize and an even more difficult thing to teach. I think we would all agree the ability to relate to one another requires empathy. For that reason, it should have a place of importance when bringing up kids. I'll tell you how my mom taught me.

I think when I first internalized empathy, I was thirteen years old. My mom, the substitute nurse at my middle school, talked to me one day about helping another student at the school. I had never even noticed Bobby before, but my mom told me he had been carrying a paper route to help pay the bills for his mother and younger sister. I reluctantly agreed, and my mom took me to his house one Tuesday afternoon to pick him up.

Even though I had lived my whole life in West Des Moines, I had never noticed Bobby's neighborhood, which seemed to me to be more like a court sentence than a place to live. His house, which would have probably fit in our garage, seemed to be leaning, and the exterior and yard were in serious disrepair.

I was not happy about knocking on his door, but I was my mother's son and had agreed. Bobby, much shorter and thinner than I, opened the door and looked at me briefly before closing the door and walking straight out to get into my mother's obnoxiously green Pontiac. My oldest brother eventually ended up with that car, and I never understood his pride in it.

The plan was to buy Bobby a pair of boots for work since his shoes were in tatters; afterward we would take him out to lunch. Kinney Shoes had a diverse selection, but it didn't take Bobby long to find the pair he was looking for. They were a light brown suede work boot, relatively popular in 1981, and would suffice as school shoes as well.

Lunch was at the Sizzler. Bobby wasn't much for talking, and he sort of hovered over his food. He ate as if he had never eaten before. I couldn't help but think it was kind of rude. His arms were on the table as he leaned over his plate; he chewed with his mouth open and answered my mother's questions as he ate, not to mention the fact he looked like he hadn't combed his hair in a few days!

When we dropped Bobby off, I didn't really say much to my mother, but I could tell she was pleased with the day's events. She asked me how I felt about the kind things we had just done for the kid. I just shrugged my shoulders. I didn't see what the big deal was. When we pulled into our driveway, before I got out of the car, she asked me to keep an eye out for him at school. Whatever.

About two weeks later, I was standing at my locker talking to a girl when I heard a commotion in Mrs. Fowler's science classroom. I opened the door and saw Bobby being chased around the desks in the dark, empty classroom by Billy Poyner. Billy was a class clown, not very bright, but his size allowed him the confidence to say and do whatever he wanted. I wouldn't say Billy and I were friends, but we had respect for one another as teammates on the same football team. Bill seemed to be toying with Bobby, who was in genuine fear for his well-being. Back in those days, the school campuses were open, and when the teachers were on break, they left their classrooms open. There were no school "deans" and little supervision in the hall, so when there was a fight, it was usually over before an adult arrived. In the dark classroom, Bill was juking one way while Bobby would head the other between the desks. The whites of Bobby's eyes told me, for him this wasn't a fun game.

"Billy!" I suggested, "Why don't you leave that kid alone?"

"What's it to you?" Billy wasn't really asking for an answer.

"Come on, man! You know Principal Beisner isn't gonna give you many more chances! That kid isn't worth it," I stated instructively.

Billy lost his enthusiasm for the chase, straightened up, and walked out of the classroom. "What's up with the party at Daniel's house this Friday, do you think Tina will be there?" he questioned me as we walked out of the classroom. I didn't say anything to Bobby. I don't think I even looked at him. I just walked upstairs to my next class, wondering why I had just intervened. I'd never even noticed that kid before. I did not know him, I'd never been around him at school, and yet for some reason I felt compelled to preserve his safety. I had nothing to gain. To my knowledge, I had never behaved in such a way before—with empathy.

What makes a person take risks to help another person? Especially a stranger. What is there to gain? The ability to lose is obvious. Seemingly, there is nothing to gain.

At one point of my life, for a college class, I wanted to run some experiments to measure empathy in people. I quickly learned from my professor it is virtually impossible to measure empathy, and here is why: let's say you witness someone falling down some stairs in a crowd of people. Some laugh, some gasp, some walk away, and some help the person up. At first glance, you might think only the gaspers and the people wanting to help are the empathetic, but you might be wrong. Helping someone who has fallen is a social norm, or at least it used to be. It's an expectation within a group of people. A person might not care at all that the other person is hurt but act out of concern for what others might think of them if they don't react appropriately. That is not empathy; it is self-preservation.

I hope that to some degree all of us are empathetic toward others. I believe we are all on an empathy spectrum. Some people are wired to care more than others. I first came to this realization when I was at a training session with a group of juvenile justice workers early in my career after I had transitioned from the military. I made a comment to a young case manager about the rest of the people in the room: "There is something similar with all of these people that I had never experienced in a group of people before." He said, "People are polarized to either giving or taking. We are the givers, and ironically, we work with the takers," referring to the juvenile delinquents we worked with. That comment turned on a switch in me that continually causes me, to this day, to tune into situations where a person is helping another person.

One of the ways we teach our foster boys to be empathetic is to have them participate in organized community service with other organizations like the Society of St. Vincent De Paul or a local gardening club. We want our boys working with other people, not just performing a task like picking up trash. Our boys routinely help clubs with older members by performing manual labor. In those cases, the club members are genuinely grateful for the help of our boys, and their honest appreciation to the kids is affirming to them. As a result, the boys feel good about themselves and hopefully internalize that not everyone can do the things they can do and that helping other people has its own reward.

As staff, we obviously show the kids empathy and often get confirmation they are learning it from us. As discussed throughout this book, many of our kids' behaviors can be extreme within the first month or so after coming to Crossroads. Often, after having been with us for six months or so, many kids will articulate that they appreciate we didn't kick them out for their behaviors or give up on them.

If you were to ask a hundred parents, "What would it take for you to disown your own son? If he committed rape? Murder? Went to prison?" I would hope 100 percent would reply that nothing would cause them to disown their own son. Realistically, I just wish 95 percent of parents felt that way.

Foster kids are uniquely denied that type of unconditional, loving relationship, and therein lies the heart of the problem with teens in the foster care system. As they move from placement to placement and take on the pain of only being cared for as long as their behaviors are good, they care less and less about their own futures. It's easier when we parent our own kids because we don't consider getting rid of them when they misbehave. Unfortunately, with foster kids, having them removed is an option if a foster parent comes to their wits' end. Being empathetic to their kids' situations and educated as to why the behaviors are happening helps a caregiver place less importance on behavioral infractions.

Appropriate Anger Expression

Boys get angry, and they usually get physical when they do. Anyone who has raised boys will tell you that. Without proper parenting, getting physical may be the only way a boy learns to express his anger, and later in life that lack of emotional maturity becomes detrimental and sometimes dangerous to society. My observations with the foster kids we have had is they tend to get in a lot fewer fights than the juvenile justice boys I previously worked with. I don't know if it is because they have a deflated ego that isn't so easily threatened or if their relationships with other boys aren't deep enough to evoke the kind of emotions that fistfights usually require.

I will tell you that our foster kids punch inanimate objects much more often than the juvenile justice boys did when they got mad. We constantly are repairing windows and door frames and sheetrock walls that have been the victims of the boys' ill-expressed anger. I remember a day when I was giving a tour to a couple of men from a church mission board. We were standing outside the education building when a boy named Anthony came charging out. He had his arms flexed in front of him and was screaming like a banshee when he went up to the first big tree he saw and gave it a one-two punch, bloodying his hands. As he walked off, I turned to the two men, who looked uneasy about the whole situation, and I reassured them there was no risk to them personally; punching the tree was the only way Anthony knew to express his anger, and with time he would learn a better way.

When we have fights between boys at Crossroads, it is usually over ill-placed comments over one of their family members. Often the fights occur during a physical activity, too, like basketball. My favorite part of working with boys rather than girls is that usually two boys will become closer friends after they have cooled off from a fight. I often joke that it's for that reason I won't work with girls. Boys can get in a fight and in twenty minutes they have forgotten about the whole thing. Girls can get in a fight and twenty years later they still have not let it go!

When we have a kid who is in a fight and having a violent anger episode, we separate him. We try to move him to a calm area where there are no other kids so he can regain his composure. After twenty minutes or so his blood pressure and breathing return to normal, and then we can start counseling and processing better ways to handle anger and instigation. De-escalation is one of my favorite times spent with kids as I can really find out who they are when they are tired and open after such an intense emotional episode. Often, in that state they will tell you things they would not otherwise tell you, and it really helps to understand who they are and why they do what they do.

Our therapists primarily work with our boys on appropriate expression of anger, but in the moment, when kids cool down after punching or kicking something, staff members are usually the ones who ask them if they could think of a better way they could have handled the situation.

Parenting

We consider the subject of parenting to be its own program at Crossroads Hope Academy. Education, culinary arts, and mental health counseling are all self-explanatory, but most people do not think of parenting as being its own program. Think about the things a normal parent has to teach: appropriate behavior, proper hygiene, nutrition, manners, not to mention all the things listed above.

Most kids grow up with caregivers who teach these things every day, albeit unintentionally and inadvertently. Sometimes a responsible caregiver will correct undesirable behavior, reward desirable behavior, require good hygiene, and teach their child how the world works. Until the age of ten most kids are around their parents almost all the time. They go to school, but when they get home and on weekends, they are being parented. Not so with teenagers. At that age they are hanging with their friends after school and on weekends and in effect are being parented by them. If you are a parent, you'd better do a good job in the younger years because that is largely all you will have!

What if a foster kid was not raised properly at a younger age or was bounced around to so many homes there was no consistency in parenting? Once they become a teenager, even though they may have a stable place to live, they have not learned the basics and are now being taught by their peers. Blind leading the blind.

At Crossroads, our staff gently correct kids when they use inappropriate language. They teach them how to clean their rooms and brush their teeth and dress appropriately. It is a daily war, but an important one. When we have a seventeen-year-old who refuses to take a shower or wash their clothes, we don't give up. We continue teaching and encouraging. At some point it eventually sinks in and they begin to make improvement, but it always requires staff continually pushing them to do better, like a parent. Honestly, when we take our boys into town for high school functions and they meet girls, that is when we see the biggest improvement in hygiene, but the groundwork still needs to be done.

Most of our kids do not know how to properly brush their teeth! Out of the 480 kids who have been through Crossroads at the date of this writing, only five have not needed major dental work when we brought them to the dentist for the first time. At this moment I have one boy who has thirty-two cavities that need to be filled!

Discipline is the trickiest skill to teach kids who largely have been very good at avoiding consequences. When we first started as a foster care home, I remember talking to a long-time foster parent who told me that when a kid goes into foster care in this country, he is handed a "victim card" and taught to be pitied for his situation. This causes the kid to learn to use that "victim card" to get out of consequences, even natural consequences, and he learns to be manipulative to get his needs met. Unlearning that "victim stance" is a difficult task.

To accomplish anything in life, a person needs self-discipline. Without being disciplined for behavior in the formative years, self-discipline is elusive as an adult. Outside the context of a relationship, disciplining a foster child is very tricky. It is the primary reason we switched our programming from the behavior modification we used in our juvenile justice days to the Collaborative Problem Solving model we use today.

When one of our boys commits a major rule infraction that warrants a behavior write-up from a staff member, a team leader or the director of operations meets with the kid one-on-one. The oversimplified version of Collaborative Problem Solving is that the adult talks with the boy about his strengths, helps him determine what he is trying to accomplish in his life at the moment through his behaviors, allows the kid to explain himself so that the adult can understand, and negotiates the consequences, ideally to the satisfaction of both parties. The process is a little more complex than that, but the idea is to build relationship and not walls between the offender and the offended.

This approach can be used in normal parenting as well, but as a parent who has a relationship with his child, there are times when standard behavior modification is more effective. As surrogate parents, we have already learned that operant conditioning, using "sticks and carrots," does not work with kids who largely have no relationships in their lives.

The Inuit Native Americans have a saying: "When you impact a person's life, you impact seven generations of his life." That means we are all products of the last two hundred years of our own heritage. When we parent our own kids, we must remember we are teaching them how to parent their kids. We feel the responsibility of that fact with our Crossroads kids as well, as it is likely that most of them will eventually be fathers too.

Chapter 9

The Daily Details

Craig

C raig came to us a wild animal. At thirteen he had more or less raised himself while his dad was in and out of jail for drugs. His mom died of an overdose when he was seven. Craig was by no means stupid, but he had not been in school for two years by the time he came to us. As a result of poor nutrition and hygiene practices, he had fourteen cavities and needed two root canals and two crowns put in. He could not sit in our school building for more than a few minutes at a time before he would run out, and those minutes were usually used disrupting the other kids.

Craig liked tools, though, and gravitated to our vocational shop. We constantly confiscated tools out of his bedroom and put them back in the shop. Craig took everything apart. He dismantled anything with screws or bolts to the point the staff were at their wits' end trying to repair things he disassembled. Craig also went out of his way to be disrespectful. He had not met a respectable adult and didn't feel he had any use for adults in general. Needless to say, our staff wanted to throw him back pretty soon after he came to us. There were a few staff members, however, who noticed his strengths.

At thirteen Craig was a much harder worker than older kids in terms of physical labor *when* we could get him engaged. Craig was easily motivated by food, so any snacks would get action from him. Additionally, he was willing to help other kids who were sad or struggling. Our vocational instructor used the fact Craig always wanted to be in the shop to motivate him to spend increasing amounts of time in math and reading. After seven months Craig was staying in school all day without disrupting classes, following rules around campus, and generally being respectful to adults. He even agreed to get his dental work done, which was a big step because he previously refused to go to the dentist even with the bribe of getting his own Apple iPad. Our team leader on the midnight-to-eight-a.m. shift had developed an amazing relationship with Craig and eventually adopted him. When he first took Craig in, most of us thought he was crazy and it wouldn't work out, but Craig, although not perfect, ended up doing well in his transition to public school because of this one relationship.

Remote Location

Craig never attempted to run away from Crossroads during his stay with us. However, many of our kids consider running from our campus when they first come. It is a seemingly easier solution to them then facing consequences for their behaviors.

The Crossroads Hope Academy campus sits on the northeast corner of a 73,000-acre ranch. Our twenty-acre campus is literally eighteen miles from the nearest business in any direction. To run away from Crossroads is a major commitment, especially in the summer when temperatures are in the mid-90s and humidity hovers near 100 percent.

I have had a few people express concerns that our foster boys are too isolated being in such a remote place. In response, I tell a story of changing behavior by reducing choices. If one of our foster boys was placed at your house in town, and you told him he needed to make his bed before he went to school, his disposition that day might cause him to run away and disappear for three days. There is little or nothing you could do to stop him.

At Crossroads a mile-long walk down a dirt road along with the view of eighteen miles of concrete in any direction usually causes the boy to come back and make his bed. After weeks of facing consequences he has previously been able to dodge, the kid learns it is not so difficult to face the music. Eventually, he even appreciates being held accountable.

I remember one afternoon as I was leaving for the day, I rolled down the window of my truck to talk to two boys who were walking down the dirt road. I asked, "What's going on, fellas?" One of the boys replied, "We're running away, Mr. John." "Do you have a plan?" I further inquired. "Yes, we have a plan—to get out of this place!" One of the boys had no shoes on, and neither of them had water or food, so I said, "Well, it's going to be a long walk without food and water." At this point they began to curse and suggested I mind my own business. I left them with this: "All right, I'll see you guys tomorrow. Have a good night." Of course, the next morning the boys were both on campus and preparing for school. I didn't play the "I told you so" card, but I tell this story often, which is satisfaction enough.

Being so far out of town also forces our kids to interact with our adult staff. This allows the opportunity for them to be parented, in many cases for the first time. At Crossroads our staff interact intentionally with our boys. They parent constantly around the clock. The boys resent it at first, but eventually they learn to depend on the parenting. You've probably heard it said before, but kids *like* structure and expectations—we all do. The simple act of encouraging better behavior while not tolerating poor behavior is truly a loving gesture.

Some parents argue that permissiveness is more loving because it is nonconfrontational. I'm here to tell you that although the intention may be loving, permissiveness is perceived as apathy, which is the opposite of love. Sometimes having too many options allows us not to grow. At Crossroads we have limited the options our kids have by housing them on a campus far from distractions.

Mental Health Counseling

Foster kids under the best circumstances still experience trauma. Data is clear that the transition between homes alone has lasting traumatic impact on kids. Over the years we have had kids come from situations you would only pray were fictional. Physical, sexual, and mental abuse. Kids who were kept in cages by their caretakers. Boys who were prostituted out by their own mothers for drugs. Quite honestly, I don't read the case files anymore. I seriously do not want to believe the level of depravity we as humans are capable of.

Many people, upon hearing about the behaviors of teens (especially this population), cannot draw the connection to why they have the capacity to act as they do. Most people only have experience with kids they have raised themselves or kids in their neighborhoods, most of whom come from what you would probably call a typical, or "normal," family. The trauma that foster kids have endured in their lives leaves them with Post Traumatic Stress Disorder (PTSD), which not only affects their behavior but also their futures if not dealt with.

At this point in history, I don't think there are many Americans who don't know what PTSD is, but perhaps not everyone is aware of how it manifests itself. According to the National Institute of Mental Health, here are some of the signs and symptoms of PTSD:

- Flashbacks—reliving the trauma over and over

- Frightening thoughts

- Nightmares or difficulty sleeping

- Avoiding feelings or thoughts about the traumatic event(s)

- Being easily startled

- Having angry outbursts

- Negative thoughts about oneself or the world

- Distorted feelings of guilt or blame

- Disruptive or destructive behaviors

A very high percentage, if not all, of foster kids have endured trauma. About 90 percent of our foster boys at Crossroads have been sexually or physically abused. They have often witnessed brutal violence and antisocial behaviors in their lives at a young and highly impressionable age. They have been shuffled from place to place and school to school. It's obvious all that trauma has a profound impact on them and their behavior.

Studies show that if a child is not bonded with a parent in early childhood development, the child is much more likely to have relational issues later in life. Additionally, he will be prone to substance abuse, have trust issues, and be learning delayed or disabled. Studies also show that every time a foster child changes placement situations, he digresses by one year in school. Foster kids are more likely to end up homeless, incarcerated, and have a much higher suicide rate than their nonfoster peers.

We would not even consider operating without mental health counselors. Our counselors do not only individual counseling with the kids but group counseling and anger therapy as well. Most of our kids agree to see the counselors, but sometimes we initially have to incentivize them to get them to go.

Over my career I have probably had two dozen mental health counselors work for me. I would estimate about half of them were ineffective or even destructive. I'm not pointing this out to disparage the industry but to highlight the importance of having the right therapists using the right therapy. Currently, we have the best group of counselors we have had in quite a few years. The kids love interacting with them, and most importantly, they will interact with the kids anywhere on campus, not just in their offices. I think that helps reduce the stigma of being in therapy for our boys. They are a younger group of therapists who play games with the kids, check up on them when not working on campus, and who from day one were never shocked by the kids' comments or actions.

Medical/ Dental/ Health Care

When we first wrote our contract as a foster home, we hadn't considered the possibility our foster kids would have the level of medical and dental problems that they do. Almost immediately after opening I had to write several grants to afford an unbudgeted position whose sole job was to run kids back and forth to the doctor and dentist. The Medicaid dentist we use will only treat one tooth per visit, further exacerbating our staffing dilemma. Of the over 480 kids we have had come through Crossroads to date, all but five have needed multiple dental problems addressed. After hearing that the first kid who came to us needed thirty-two cavities filled, I remember telling the boy, "I'm pretty sure you only have thirty-two teeth!" We have a fourteen-year-old right now that needs seventeen cavities filled, two root canals, and a crown put on. In his case, just convincing him to go is a struggle. Imagine being told you were going to have to go to the dentist twice per week for the next three months!

The visits to the doctor for physical checkups aren't much more encouraging. Many of our kids suffer from hypertension, are prediabetic, or need more tests to determine the reasons for their poor health. The stress of instability coupled with poor hygiene and diet are almost certainly to blame. Additionally, I would say that consistently 50 percent of our kids are on psychotropic drugs for various mental health diagnoses.

Years ago the *Miami Herald* did a story about how foster kids are overmedicated compared to their peers coming from nonfoster settings. Legislators would espouse the evils of putting foster kids on psychotropics and passed laws making it more difficult to do so by physicians. The first psychiatrist I contracted with left after three months because of those laws. He told me, "John, I'm not going to ask a lawyer for permission to fulfill the duties of my job."

Personally, after doing this for so many years, I can honestly say I'm not sure what the alternative could be to prescribing medications. Our kids' diets have been terrible before they come to us, their lives have been chaotic, and with the trauma they have endured throughout their lives, I'm not sure a psychiatrist in an hour a month has any other option besides prescribing medication.

To briefly address diet, when I first hired our food services supervisor, Ms. Shelly, she told me she wanted to get rid of our deep fat fryer in the kitchen and plant a garden out back. She was already well aware of the damage processed and fatty foods have on young growing bodies, and she wanted to introduce fresh produce and reduced-fat and low-sugar foods to bring back some health to our boys. At Crossroads we are careful about what we feed them, and Shelly often hides vegetables in the things they would normally eat, like mashed potatoes and macaroni and cheese.

Church

As Christians we obviously believe participation with a local body of believers is important for our kids. As a partially state-funded agency, we also understand the delicacy of the presentation of religion to those we care for. From the beginning, we have had several churches participate with us in our mission. They come to serve food to the boys on weekends, play basketball and games with them, conduct weekly Bible studies, and even hold Sunday services. Additionally, some of our staff will pick kids up on the weekend to take them to their own churches. We also take the kids who want to attend to a local youth group on Wednesday nights and to Sunday services when the staffing allows it.

I would guess 90 percent or more of our volunteers are church-attending Christians, so the kids also have that exposure. Having said that, we are cognizant the church is imperfect and that many of our kids have been hurt by so-called believers during their foster experiences. For those reasons, we are careful in choosing the volunteers who come in contact with our kids, considering how they will involve faith in their interactions.

I remember one of our first kids at Crossroads could not be placed with his younger sister because the Mennonite family who adopted her did not want him. That made Austin truly angry and bitter not only toward

Christians but also God. We had another kid whose Jewish foster parents would discipline him by locking him in a closet. That kid would get visibly upset anytime the subject of God came up. Understandably so.

In most translations of the Bible, the third commandment of the Ten Commandments says, "You shall not take the name of the LORD your God in vain" (Exodus 20:7). The version that I prefer says: "You shall not *carry* the Lord's name in vain" (emphasis mine). My guess is there is probably a special place in hell for people who profess to be children of God but inflict harm on others as representatives of him. Especially if those they are inflicting harm on are vulnerable foster kids!

When I speak to religious organizations and churches, I always bring up this verse: "Religion that God our Father accepts as pure and faultless is this: to look after orphans and widows in their distress and to keep oneself from being polluted by the world" (James 1:27 NIV). As a person who spends a great deal of time recruiting assistance from the church, I could probably write a whole book just on that one verse. The English Standard Version (ESV) of James 1:27 says "to *visit* orphans and widows" (emphasis mine). I always bring that up when I'm speaking at a church because many people are uncertain about their own ability to work with teens.

I usually ask people just to come and have lunch with the boys. I tell them about a couple who attended our Christmas party a few years back. I saw them sitting at a back table with our newest kid, whom I knew very little about at the time. At the end of the Christmas party, they came up to me and said, "We just love that kid! Can we come out on Tuesday to have lunch with him?" That led to weekly lunches and then texting and phone calls and then getting their background screenings done so he could go off campus with them until finally he was spending weekends with them. Years later they still communicate with him weekly as if he was one of their own sons. That all started with a "visit" to an orphan.

I suspect if I would have asked them to mentor the boy that first night at the Christmas party, they would have told me they didn't have time, but that is what they ended up doing. They have made an incredible impact on the young man, and it all started with a simple meal with him. Incidentally, that same couple is currently beginning a relationship with another one of our boys. They missed the interactions they had had with Corey.

When I invite people to come out to our campus for a tour or to have lunch with the boys, I'm obviously hoping to make lifelong friends for Crossroads kids. My primary motive, however, is to have them interact with the boys so that the boys will feel loved. Stepping into your local high school cafeteria to show a little attention to those kids might have a minimal impact. However, just coming to Crossroads sends the message to our boys that they are not forgotten and they have value. I know this because the kids have told me so. Recently, I told a group of volunteers, who came out to prepare supper and hang out with the kids, that their monthly presence makes a visible and substantial impact on the whole Crossroads culture. A few of them responded they themselves were the ones who benefited by serving the boys and talking with them. That is encouraging.

Community Service

Having foster kids participate in community service might seem strange to some people, but I personally believe giving to and helping others not only is healing but is an integral part of a healthy life and builds a strong community. I can honestly say I have witnessed transformation in our boys after they have participated in community service projects. I don't want to oversimplify, but I'd like you just to think for a moment about a person who believes he is worthless. His family has abandoned him, and other foster families have given up on him. He carries his possessions around in a black garbage bag. What would you think of yourself in that situation? Now take that same person working alongside a retiree who is helping to build a community garden. The retiree turns to the boy, pats him on the shoulder, looks him in the eye, and gives honest appreciation for his help. The message to that boy is "You matter." For you and me that may not be so impactful, but to a foster kid it's like throwing a life preserver to a drowning man.

I don't allow our kids to get involved in community service that doesn't have a human component, such as picking up trash on the side of the road. While that activity is valuable, I worry that it might send the wrong message to my kids, and it clearly wouldn't have the same impact on them as one where they are working alongside an adult.

One of the boys' favorite community service activities is working monthly in the local St. Vincent de Paul's community yard sale. Our boys help elderly people carry and load their purchases into their cars. The boys feel valued by those people and often even get tips. The St. Vincent de Paul staff love the help, and they always let the kids pick out something for themselves and then feed them before they return to campus. I have been caught off guard when giving a tour of the campus only to open a bedroom door and see a Tiffany-style stained glass table lamp or Renoir knockoff painting on the wall! I have seen some funny "treasures" over the years as well. Despite the early Saturday morning start time for the yard sale, the kids love being part of the event.

We also like to involve our kids in events that help stretch their experiences. We participate in an annual themed chili cook-off where the kids dress up in costumes and help decorate the serving tent. We have even won trophies at that event, also a first for most of our kids. We have helped the local Rotary and Kiwanis Clubs set up and break down for their fundraisers, as well as helped churches with their weekend events.

Education

During our time as a juvenile justice program, we got in a pretty successful rhythm of working with kids who were largely truant and uninterested in school prior to coming to us. Our classrooms looked similar to public schools with a much smaller class size and a slightly more hands-on approach to learning. In our model, we were consistently seeing academic gains of a year and a half to two years of improvement in math and reading during the kids' compulsory six-month stays with us. In that model, however, we controlled the one thing that the kids wanted: when they could go home. Our rank structure had clearly defined benchmark requirements, and one of those was a requirement for quality participation in educational classes. Kids eventually buckled down because they realized it was the only way they were going to be able to go home.

When we took our first foster kids in after closing as a juvenile justice facility, we assumed they would do as well as our juvenile justice kids in that model. We were wrong. We were shocked to discover our boys had not consistently been in school for an average of two years. I remember one thirteen-year-old who had not walked across the threshold of a school building for more than two years! Our kids were not dumb; they were just extremely behind in their studies. Our testing demonstrated that the average reading level among our twelve- to eighteen-year-olds was the first month of fifth grade.

Every year, we changed our programming a little to try to figure out what worked best with the foster boys. Having a teacher instruct in the front of the room didn't work at all! Teaching this unique population is difficult. We tried combinations of teachers prescribing work and demonstrating problem solving along with online classes. Eventually we settled on complete online classes, for a few reasons. The most important reason was that more than 50 percent of our kids are transitory; we average fifty-five kids per year for a twenty-four-bed foster home. It is much easier for them to resume their classes seamlessly in an online setting when moving from place to place than for schools to have to figure out which textbook they were using at their previous school. Secondly, we found there is more support for the online classes. The teachers of those classes are available for assistance by chat, Zoom, or phone, along with our classroom instructors. And then there is the cost of degreed teachers as opposed to having trained classroom aids.

As a juvenile justice program, we were protected by a state law that required the school system to pay full-time equivalent (FTE) funding to help supplement the cost of our educational component. When we became a foster home, the superintendent of Charlotte County Schools came and asked us to apply to become a charter school so they could legally continue funding us. So we did. We got a lot of media attention as a charter school. We even had a graduate! It was a first for Crossroads, so we held the graduation at a church in town, with about sixty people in attendance, including a school board member. We did the graduation right, with a cap and gown, and we even played "Pomp and Circumstance" as the graduate walked to receive his diploma. Felix will always be able to say he was the first person ever to graduate from Crossroads Hope Academy. After four years, we terminated our charter, but even if we were to have remained a charter school, it is not likely we would have had many graduates. The kids we receive are educationally deficient and academically so far behind, they are usually unable to catch up their credits before the age of eighteen.

Eventually the requirements for charter schools in Florida became so restrictive, when it came time to reapply, our board of directors decided it would be best for us to go it alone. Two main restrictions enacted by the Florida Legislature and the Department of Education brought us to that decision. One was the requirement to demonstrate educational gains on an annual basis, and the second was the requirement to have a School Resource Officer (SRO) on site.

Charter schools were given a free reign for a lot of years in Florida until 2018 when legislation passed that held charter schools accountable for the academic progress of their students. At Crossroads we realized we would never be able to consistently demonstrate annual academic gains in a foster home with such high student turnover rates. In four years of being a charter school, the most students we ever had complete the entire school year with us was six. Even getting our kids to take the state-mandated tests was challenging, especially the newer kids. We even tried "incentivizing" them with sodas and chips, but that only worked marginally. Demonstrating academic gains over the long haul would clearly be impossible for us.

The Parkland High School shooting happened in February of 2018 in Parkland, Florida. In a knee-jerk reaction, the legislation passed a law starting July 1 of the same year requiring all public schools to have a School Resource Officer on site, at a cost of about $100,000 annually. This included charter schools. The law passed without taking into consideration that during the Parkland High School shooting incident, the School Resource Officer was not helpful in the prevention or de-escalation of the incident. Frustrated, my board and I petitioned our local legislators and the Department of Education at the state level, but to no avail.

One email I sent to the Commissioner of Education was descriptive of the fact that our kids lived with us twenty-four hours per day and that requiring us to have a resource officer on site for five hours a day, 180 days out of the year didn't even have a meaningful impact on the safety of our kids. The email I received back only reiterated the department's concern for the kids during the school day. Bureaucracy!

Education is not the first thing on a foster kid's mind when he comes to us. When I speak to groups of people, I often use Maslow's Hierarchy of Needs to explain our struggles with moving kids forward educationally. When our kids first come to us, they don't really know where they are going to sleep or when they are going to eat, so concern for their own education is far down the list of priorities. For most of our kids, we don't see meaningful production in the classroom until months after they arrive. The thirteen-year-old I was telling you about above, Craig, had been living in the streets of St. Petersburg since the age of ten. He hadn't been in a school since the age of eleven. When he came to us in February, he wouldn't sleep at night but just sat awake with the night staff.

In the mornings, my staff would drag him to the school building where he would sleep all day. By the end of the semester however, he was on the honor roll. We had to learn about Craig's issues and then help him with them. He was afraid of the dark and had trust issues. Until we made a few adjustments in his sleeping arrangements, he would not go to bed at night. But after a few months of our consistent behavior, predictable structure, and relationship building, he came around and really began focusing on his future.

New kids not wanting to participate in education has been the norm for us. However, sometimes we have kids who have an affinity for education even if they are behind their peers academically. For some kids, school was a safe place psychologically as they were growing up, and it shows in their eagerness to participate. The longer kids stay at Crossroads, the more educational work we get out of them and consequently they demonstrate greater educational gains.

Over the years, we have averaged four kids getting their GEDs annually. Our policy is to keep them going after they obtain their GED, so most of those kids enroll in college immediately following receiving their diploma. We take our graduates for a tour of the local college (Florida Southwestern State College), and usually just seeing all the girls can get a commitment from them to attend.

In Florida, state tuition is free for foster kids, so there is little expense to cover while they are still living with us. Our donors are eager to cover the ancillary costs of our kids going to college. The kids who attend college also become an inspiration to the other Crossroads kids. Very few of our kids have a family member with college experience, so getting a degree can seem out of reach to them. While they are with us, we can tutor them to help ensure their early success. Over the years we have also had a few kids attend vocational school and a few who just wanted to work, but we always insist on not letting them just sit around after their high school career is over.

Sadly, to date, not one of the kids who have been at Crossroads has completed their college degree. Nationally, only 60 percent of all kids entering college complete their bachelor's degree at the same university they start, but foster kids' completion rates are much lower. Only 2 percent of foster kids enter college after high school. Compare that to about 69 percent of their peers who enter college after high school. Our experience is that if we are able to get a kid into a short-term vocational school or working in a job where he is taught a skilled trade, his chances of achieving stability are greatly improved.

Crossroads Cantina

A local church decided they would develop a vacant space in one of our buildings into a "store" for the boys. Their members built out the store and raised money for the air conditioning, carpeting, a refrigerator, display racks and cases, and a changing room. Eighteen miles from the nearest gas station, Crossroads is ideally located for our programming, but that leaves little opportunity for kids to buy their own snacks, hygiene items, clothes, and other things. The church members maintain the store, and our staff opens it three times per week so the kids can spend their "Crossroads bucks" on items they want.

They earn their bucks through various positive behaviors or academic achievements, and there is no actual cash or tickets exchanged. Their earnings are accounted for in a binder by our staff, as we have learned that handing kids tokens, or "bucks," causes all manner of problems. The store is definitely not a new idea, but the kids are particularly proud of it, and they have input as to what is stocked. Our location makes it difficult for younger kids to earn real money beyond their allowance, so the store is particularly valuable to them. Our older kids often work in town at local businesses, but they don't take any less interest in the store.

Allowance

We give our kids a weekly graduated allowance based on behavior. The minimum a kid can earn weekly is five dollars. If he misses no school, attends counseling, and has completed all his chores and kept his room clean, he could earn ten or even fifteen dollars per week. For most of the kids, it is enough to pay their monthly cell phone bills. Unfortunately, it isn't as big of a motivator as you might think for reasons discussed throughout this book.

Cell Phones

The Crossroads staff have a love/hate relationship with kids having cell phones. Many of our kids are from outside our county and keeping in touch with family and friends from previous schools is only possible through the use of cell phones. They can be disruptive, however. We have had kids call for Uber rides to run away or order pizzas, and we have even had kids call drug dealers to bring drugs to them on campus. Additionally, kids will often film each other or film something inappropriate and then upload that to the internet. In Florida, it is illegal for kids to be identified publicly as foster kids. Some of our kids' families are not allowed to know where they are for the sake of their safety. You can imagine the trouble it causes us as staff members when the kids share information online about their whereabouts. We have had kids call 911 if they felt bullied or had their property stolen by another boy, but we have reached an agreement with the sheriff's department that they would only respond to a call in our part of the county if they heard from a staff member directly.

Kids' Possessions

When we initially opened, we bought wooden dressers for the kids' belongings. What we didn't anticipate in that decision is how much some of the kids would try to steal from others. Additionally, those dressers could not handle the level of wear our boys were able to inflict. We went to the local custom auto shop and had them build truck boxes on wheels with sturdy hasp locks that could be locked so each kid would have his own steel truck box. The kids eventually learned how to break the hasps, however, so for a long time we still experienced kids getting their things messed with.

Our director of operations and our business manager did some exhaustive research, and we had a few donors give us enough money to buy each kid a floor safe. That way they could keep their clothes in the truck box but keep their personal things in the floor safe. We needed safes that we had master control over in case the kid forgot his code or was storing something inappropriate. We ended up purchasing safes that could be programed to accept a thumbprint for opening. The kids learned that by putting a piece of cellophane over the print reader and then placing their thumb on top, the safes would open. Once again, we were searching for a solution to kids having their things stolen! My thought was to approach a safe company to see if they would try their newest products on our kids just to see how invincible they are.

From the beginning of our endeavor, I always thought it was strange our kids would show up with all their possessions in a black plastic garbage bag. At this point, I think it is the most egregious thing to see in the national foster care system. At first, it enraged me to see it. Why weren't caregivers getting these kids luggage or something proper to keep their belongings in?

At about the sixth-month mark of being open, we had a boy turning eighteen, and the transporter was scheduled to come from Tampa on a certain day. We had his birthday party and Crossing Over ceremony all set up for that evening with dozens of volunteers coming all the way to campus to help celebrate.

The morning of the birthday party the transporter showed up to collect Ronald and all his things. They hadn't called us to say she was coming early to get him; she just showed up. I called her boss, then her boss's boss to explain that we take the eighteenth-birthday ceremony especially seriously and we had already agreed they would not get him until the following day. After forty-five minutes of frustrating discussion, we relented to let him leave. When I asked Ronald if he had suitcases and he indicated he did not, the transporter said, "We usually just put their stuff in garbage bags." I lost my cool: "Just because that is the norm doesn't make it right!"

Our kids come to us after being discarded by their previous foster placements and, in some cases, by their parents. We didn't need to perpetuate a norm that puts their possessions in the same black plastic bag where we put everything else we don't want. When I described this injustice in my weekly newsletter, more than a hundred used suitcases showed up on my step, donated by people. It got to the point I had to tell them to stop because we didn't have the space anymore to store them. As far as the birthday party went for Ronald, my volunteers met him in the Winn Dixie parking lot in town to let him blow out his candles and to give him his presents before he got on the interstate with his transporter. It was our least impressive birthday celebration.

I noticed over time that very few of our kids came with any real personal possessions. If I had to guess, I would say that less than 10 percent of the kids who come to us have anything personal with them when they show up. Everything they bring is handed down or given to them at the places they have stayed. Very few kids come with family photos, toys, knickknacks, jewelry, or for that matter anything other than clothes and hygiene items. I find it interesting that foster kids, who have lost every person in their lives, place little value on the things in their lives, at least not enough value to hold on to those things as they move from place to place.

You and I, on the other hand, probably have lots of things we are particularly concerned about. Personally, I don't like people even touching my guitars, and when I discovered one of my more expensive ones had suffered damage caused by humidity and needed extensive structural work, I almost threw up! I probably need to adjust the sense of value I place on my "things."

One of the first kids who came to Crossroads brought a guitar, and later another kid maliciously threw it in the firepit. I was more upset than the kid whose guitar got destroyed. It astonishes me that foster teens don't consider their possessions that important, but maybe I'm the one who needs to modify his priorities. The kids place more value on people, the ones they have lost, than on things, whether they've had them or not.

After one birthday party, the volunteer who'd wrapped the kid's presents (a separate donor had paid for them) was very upset that he gave his most expensive gift to another kid. She said to me, "Why don't we not buy the kids gifts and just have the party?" I told her the donor who pays for the gift is primarily concerned the kid has a special day and presents are part of that. Once the kid opens his present, it belongs to him. What he does with it is his choice. I do admit, though, when I see the kids get nice things for their birthdays or Christmas, I tend to assume those things won't last very long.

Administrative Responsibilities

I obviously did not get into the "business" of stewarding other people's children for business's sake. There are much easier ways to make money with a lot less responsibility! That being said, I think it is important if I am going to write a book on Crossroads Hope Academy to talk about the real-world connectivity and functioning of running the business side of the "business." Also, I get a lot of questions when I speak to groups about these particular "nuts and bolts."

When a child is accepted to Crossroads, our business manager (Ms. Tina) is notified. The placing agency sends a rate agreement that usually is taken from our contract with our lead agency in Fort Myers (Children's Network of Southwest Florida). We take kids from around the state, so if we bring in a kid who is not in the Sunshine Health network of Medicaid, there is an extra charge until the kid's caseworker can get him moved to our version of Medicaid. That usually takes them about a month.

We found out early on that if we did not demand the higher rate upon acceptance of a kid, the placing agencies would have no incentive to get the required forms filled out so we could get the kid medical and dental attention. Crossroads does not bill Medicaid anymore, as that process has become ridiculously laborious, but our local doctors, dentists, and therapists all bill the Sunshine Health network within Medicaid.

Ms. Tina and Ms. Charity, our case manager, work together to bill the placing agencies monthly. We work with fourteen of the seventeen placing agencies that exist in Florida, which means there are fourteen different methods of billing and payment. It can be frustrating.

In addition, Ms. Tina, along with Ms. Shelly, accounts for and bills the National School Lunch program (NSLP). The NSLP reimburses us for about 75 percent of the cost of our meals. Anyone associated with receiving funding from a federal source knows there are excessive amounts of documents required at the time of billing.

Per our contract, we are required to provide monthly information on each of our kids to each of the placing agencies. Most of that information comes from Ms. Charity and through our treatment team process, but we also provide medical, dental, and therapy intervention information about each of the kids to each of the placing agencies. If a kid has juvenile justice charges or other court sanctions, then Ms. Charity also communicates with those entities monthly. Informally, guardian ad litems, family members, and caseworkers call almost daily to find out how their kids are doing at Crossroads. There are days when the phone literally doesn't stop ringing. I've joked that Ms. Charity is the "air traffic controller" of information at Crossroads.

Annually, we are audited for licensure by the Department of Children and Families (DCF) and the Children's Network, our lead contracted Community Based Care (CBC) organization provider. They look at our financial practices, employee files (including background screening requirements and training), our physical facility, medication administration, and our case files for each of the kids, both past and present. They also do interviews with both youth and staff.

Background screening requirements on each of the staff requires Ms. Tina to get local, state, and federal background checks done on each of the staff annually. Additionally, she has to get a sex-offender registry check done on each staff annually and a 911 call check from each of the cities and counties where our twenty-four staff members live. It is extensive. We also pay to have an external audit of our finances done to demonstrate good financial oversight of our organization. We have an annual fire inspection and an annual health inspection of the facility, and the health inspector comes out quarterly as well as randomly throughout the year to inspect our cafeteria and living spaces. We also have an annual accreditation self-assessment we must provide to the Council on Accreditation (COA). They come for a site visit every four years.

Our medications must be stored behind two locked storage receptacles. Controlled substances must be counted every day by two people. When medications are handed out, the administering staff and the kid both have to initial that the pill was given and received. Any discrepancy must be dealt with immediately and aggressively. We have a pharmacist who comes to Crossroads monthly both to oversee our medication storage and to remove any discarded or expired medications.

Something you may not know is that you are not supposed to flush medications, once they expire or are no longer needed, down the toilet or throw them in the trash, as they negatively impact the environment. Most fire stations have a location to dispose of unwanted medications. Here is the thing, though, it is not legally allowed to be in possession of someone else's controlled substance medications. That means if I were to try to drive those discarded medications to the fire station myself and I got pulled over, I could go to jail.

We are accredited through the Council on Accreditation (COA). The sheer volume of information they want to see, from policies and procedures to supervision logs, is astounding! There are 430 indicators for which we must provide documents demonstrating to them that we are complying with their standards for excellence as well as with our contracts and state law. Fortunately, the on-site visit only takes place every four years because the preparation for the visit takes over a month just collecting all the information they require to see. Our first ever site visit took a year and a half to prepare for. The end result of being nationally accredited is it gives us instant credibility as an entity to outside agencies who may consider working with us.

Then there are donations. We have all seen directors of nonprofits go to jail over the slightest mishandling of finances. The smallest cash donation requires handling by two people. Then the donation acknowledgment letter, properly formatted, must be sent to the donor, and the donation must be properly documented in our accounting system.

In-kind donations must be handled properly too. A volunteer once came to me and said she would never donate again to the local Homeless Coalition because she had donated a KitchenAid mixer and when she went back the next week, was told someone on staff had taken it home. The executive director was a friend of mine, and when I told her the story, she looked into it. It wasn't true that the staff member took the donated machine home, but the damage in reputation had been done, and who knows with how many people our volunteer shared her story.

After one hurricane season, I had a staff member bury the front end of his car driving down our dirt road when he attempted to drive through what he thought was a puddle. The recent hurricane created what was actually a six-foot-deep trough in our road. His car was totaled. At the time, I had several donated vehicles intended to be given to kids when they aged out of foster care. I asked my board if I could give my staff member one of the donated cars; then I got ahold of one of the donors who I knew wouldn't mind about the car and asked him as well. I then got written permission from the donor before I made the transfer. These are the kinds of decisions a nonprofit director must be very careful about.

The board of directors is technically my boss (or bosses). It might sound exhausting to have twelve bosses, but with the right people on the board, it is quite reassuring to have them. That being said, there are days when our board members require a lot of time from both me and Tina. At the time of this writing, we have the best board I have ever worked with in twenty-seven years of nonprofit work. Each person has their specific areas of expertise, and they all take their responsibility of stewardship of our foster home seriously. Not only can each of our board members recite our mission, but most of them also helped write it! I would guess that on any given day of the week, I have a conversation with at least one board member.

Our accreditation auditors reported to me that they were very impressed with the commitment and dedication of our board members. Those people work with hundreds of nonprofits around the country, so it was quite a compliment.

We have monthly board meetings, and they are always lively. Our board is not made up of people who look forward to "meeting to meet." They are constantly pushing to help us get to the next level in all areas. In fact, the writing of this book was the idea and almost a mandate of our past board chair because he intuitively knew most people have no idea what the deep end of the foster care system looks like.

The regular day-to-day business of Crossroads is like riding a roller coaster. We have great staff, but if one calls in sick or, God forbid, suddenly quits without notice, we have to scramble to cover the shifts. Our contract says we will not have any more than six kids to each staff member on each shift. With our kind of kids, I would be much more comfortable with 1 staff member to four kids, if we could afford it. If for some reason we were not in proper staff-to-youth ratio and had an incident, we could be setting ourselves up for a lawsuit.

I started out in 1995 as a direct-care staff member. I never considered back then that I would find myself managing the entire operations of a human services organization, but here I am. The administrative side of a non-profit organization is not as immediately rewarding as the operations side, but it has its days. I often encourage my staff that they are the ones who change kids' lives for the better not me, I am only support for them.

SECTION V

Hindsight and Foresight

Chapter 10

You Probably Haven't Thought About This

Shane

At fourteen, Shane had the sad temperament of a person who had lost all hope. His honest and sweet demeanor made him easy to like. But Shane had another side: an explosive temper that was largely unpredictable. Shane broke his forearm playing touch football with the other kids. The doctor told him he would not be able to use the arm for six weeks and forbade him from participating in sports. Shane complied for about a day. Shane came to the window of our management meeting and began pounding on it with his cast. If it wasn't a hurricane-impact window, Shane would have added lacerations to his present injury. He was mad because the staff wouldn't let him play football with the other kids. It was useless to talk to him; he was manic. After Shane calmed down, Bo, our director of operations, negotiated with him explaining again what he could and couldn't do physically. A process he had to repeat almost every day for the duration of the time that the cast was on his arm.

Feast and Famine

When we were preparing to write our contract to become a foster home and school in Florida, we discovered we would be paid a daily per-diem rate for each kid. Previously, we worked with a contracted facility rate under the department of juvenile justice that wasn't dependent on how many kids we had in our program. The main problem with a daily rate of pay per number of kids is that staffing ratios are required through state statute and therefore an expensive fixed cost. We carefully plotted out our budget for the new endeavor and counted on having nineteen kids in our twenty-four-bed facility daily.

After we opened, the kids trickled in, and my case manager and I had to drive around the state and talk to placing agencies to let them know who we were and that we were an open and available resource to accept kids. Soon enough, as our costs weren't being covered by our wavering enrollment, it didn't look like we would survive long. It took almost six months to fill our ranks to the nineteen kids we needed to cover our bills. Over that period of time, we went through $600,000 in savings! As it turns out, we seriously miscalculated the cost of care for our boys, making us dependent on fund-raising to close the gap. That initial miscalculation was a blessing however because there is no way my board at the time would have signed up for a deficit budget.

One of the things we least expected was the transiency of the kids in foster care in the state of Florida. On average, we were losing one boy per week. They were moved by the courts, or by their case managers, or got themselves in trouble and were removed from Crossroads. To this day, that rate of attrition still stands. Regardless, it meant we had to enroll more than one kid per week if we were ever going to be full. The side effects of bringing in too many boys too quickly, however, is having absolute chaos among the kids.

Historically, Crossroads has had at least one event per year where we would lose four or five kids at once, either from one incident or coincidentally by rapid attrition. When that happens, it takes us about six months to catch up. From the beginning, we have received plenty of referrals from placing agencies (we are currently averaging eighty per month), but we have learned that if we bring in too many kids all at once, we have mayhem. New kids who are with us under a month make up the bulk of our negative statistics: running away, fights, Baker Acts, drugs, etc. Worse than that, they almost always cause some of our long-term kids to fall in with their negative behaviors, causing those kids to regress socially and emotionally. One step forward, two steps back.

When we were a juvenile justice facility, I used to ask the kids in a group setting how many of them had stolen a car or had broken into someone's home *on their own*. No one ever raised their hands. They always were with other kids and collectively decided to make a bad decision. The same process happens with our foster boys.

There is a line in the movie *Men in Black* that I used to tell the kids. Regarding extra-terrestrial life on earth, Will Smith says to Tommy Lee Jones, "Why the big secret? People are smart. They can handle it." Tommy Lee says, "A person is smart. People are dumb, panicky, dangerous animals, and you know it." That exact reason is why we like to bring kids in slowly. It has a much less radical impact on our student culture.

For several years we sent our boys to a Christian summer camp for a week in June. We never had an incident until the last year. The camp let their supervision get a little lax and ended up calling the sheriff on nineteen kids, five of whom were ours. When the dust settled, we didn't get those five kids back, and it took six months to get fully enrolled again. All the while, we were using up savings to survive.

When COVID-19 hit and the nation went into quarantine, we didn't take any kids in for six weeks, but we still had attrition. By the time we got down to fourteen, we had to start bringing in kids rapidly because we also didn't have much of an ability to fund-raise during the pandemic. In the first month of the quarantine, we had the least amount of behavior reports than we had ever had. By July, however, after bringing in nine kids in five weeks, we had the most behavior reports we had ever had in one month. The staff were worn out too. This is yet another example to emphasize the importance of stability when placing foster kids.

Grievances

Most organizations have a policy or methodology that allows people to voice their concerns and get resolution. Crossroads is no different. Over the years we have had some doozies too! I take them all seriously though because I figure if they wrote it down, they were serious about wanting resolution to their issue. At least they were at the time of writing the grievance.

Our grievance policy requires the boys follow the chain of command until resolution has occurred. The team leader will sit and discuss the kid's grievance with him, and if it is resolved, it goes no further. However, if the author of the grievance isn't satisfied or if the complaint is about the team leader, the director of operations meets with the boy. If the grievance still isn't resolved or the complaint is about the director of operations, then the executive director meets with the boy. Beyond that, the board would get involved, but we have never had a grievance go that far. Let me tell you about the most recent grievance I received to illustrate how frustrating the process can be.

On a Saturday, the air conditioning unit in one of our dorms shut down. The team leader sent a voice text to Ms. Tina, our business manager. That's significant because a voice text does not give a notification that a text has been received like a regular text does, so our business manager did not even know she was contacted until hours later. When she finally noticed the voice text, she called the team leader to ask if he had tried vacuuming out the condensation drain line of the air conditioning unit. He hadn't, so she reminded him how.

The next day, the team leader who comes in on Sundays called Ms. Tina to tell her the AC unit wasn't working. Apparently the first team leader had not called back to say he was unable to get it running. Again, Ms. Tina explained how to vacuum the drain line, and the team leader called back to say it was working. Later, however, the AC quit again, and Tina called the AC company to come out and fix it, which they did.

The Friday before, a staff member poured bleach down the drain line on the AC unit in cottage one. It's a fairly standard way to keep the drain lines clean and something we have been doing for years. Misinformation ensued between staff and kids like the old "telephone" game where people pass information by whispering around in a circle and in the end the message sounds nothing like how it began.

Monday morning, I came into the office to see five grievances on my desk from kids claiming the director of operations (who had nothing to do with the entire event) was incompetent, the staff were throwing bleach into the AC unit (wrong unit, uninformed purpose), the cottage was ninety degrees (the high that day was seventy-four degrees and rainy), and no one cared about the well-being of the kids.

The kids were grateful I met with them. It proved to them the grievance process works and we all have appreciation for their concerns. However, I used the meetings as a teaching moment to demonstrate how information can get so far out of whack and can create anger and confusion. I used the same illustration with the staff and suggested they keep kids informed as things develop so they don't escalate into a situation where kids feel mistreated.

Over the years we have probably had fewer than twenty grievances from kids. Few have made it all the way to me. The main point of going through the process is to allow the kids to have a voice and to know we take them seriously.

Child Abuse Hotline

I think this subject will interest most of you. Over the years I have heard many people say the number one reason they won't consider taking in a foster kid is they are worried the kid might falsely accuse them of abuse and it would be detrimental to their life. Many times, kids call the child abuse hotline because it gives them a sense of control, but it doesn't change the fact that the fallout from the call can be disastrous for adults.

A youth pastor called me to ask about the ins and outs of the foster care system and about fostering, as he and his wife were considering taking in foster teens. He had heard there was a great need for foster homes for teens and he and his wife thought they could help. I cautioned him that I had no experience with the "run of the mill" foster kids and I could only paint him a worst-case scenario since my boys happened to be particularly challenging. My comments also included that he needed to be committed because many foster teens resent being parented.

His main concern was being accused by a child and then having that becoming detrimental to his personal and work life. I told him he could almost certainly count on the accusation. Teens do not like to be disciplined, and a phone call to the abuse hotline is the easiest way to buy relief from consequences. I know of several cases where an accusation has landed an adult in a difficult situation.

A former staff member of mine can no longer work around kids in any capacity because of an accusation by a seventeen-year-old. A Crossroads board member and I spent considerable time trying to reverse the state's decision through appeal but to no avail. If that staff member would have been more detailed in the write-up of the incident or had another adult around him when the interaction with the youth took place, he wouldn't have lost a seven-year career with Crossroads and wouldn't be in a position now where he can't work around kids.

About once a year, we need to have a kid removed from Crossroads because of the allegations he makes against staff. It is sad when we have to do that to protect our operations, but it is a consequence of an imperfect reporting system. Mandatory reporting laws require case managers, youth workers, medical staff, and law enforcement officials to call the Florida Abuse Hotline if a suspected abuse has occurred. The Abuse Hotline is a state-run agency which accepts reports, twenty-four hours a day, seven days a week, 365 days a year, of known or suspected child abuse, neglect, or abandonment, and reports of known or suspected abuse, neglect, or exploitation of a vulnerable person.

We recently had a thirteen-year-old tell his case manager the Crossroads staff would not let him eat and that is why he hadn't gained weight. The case manager called the Abuse Hotline and the next day a Child Protective Investigator (CPI) came to see if there was any truth to the allegation. There was not. The reality is, there are no consequences for the youth making the claim, and the abuse report stays open for up to sixty days. That means anyone with a computer can easily see that Crossroads has a pending abuse investigation, regardless of validity.

This can affect placements being made, as some placing agencies have policies about not sending kids to places with open abuse investigations. Worse still, if a staff member is listed by name, it is possible the staff member won't be able to work around kids in any fashion until the case is closed. That could mean being placed on unpaid administrative leave for two months.

Additionally, several of our current staff are coaches and youth leaders in the community and in their churches. The background requirements of those positions mandate they wouldn't be allowed around kids there until an open abuse investigation case is closed. Again, two months.

We have had kids claim sexual misconduct, physical abuse, and medical neglect by staff and our facility. We even had a kid call the Abuse Hotline because we wouldn't let him have dessert without eating some of his meal first! Fortunately, Crossroads has not had any *founded* claims against it as of the date of this writing. Is there room for policy and regulation improvement? Probably.

Sometimes after a kid leaves our facility, they will make a claim requiring a mandatory reporter to make the phone call to the Abuse Hotline. Sometimes the allegations require the legal system to become involved and the sheriff shows up on our doorstep to hand out subpoenas to both kids and adults, ordering them to appear in court. At the current moment, I am dealing with exactly that situation.

This morning I arrived on campus to have a deputy hand out five subpoenas to kids and seven to staff members. This happens about once every three or four months, and we always have to call the state's attorney to reduce the number of adults who receive a subpoena so we can continue with operations.

I'm not advocating for restricting the Abuse Hotline. It is an unfortunate necessity. However, false accusations can have lasting negative consequences for caregivers, yet they have no consequences for accusers. We have had staff quit because they were worried an investigator might make a mistake in a false accusation. A founded abuse accusation would greatly impact their ability to work around kids in the future.

We have learned to be very careful around new kids especially. Rarely if ever do we allow one staff to be around one youth with no other supervision. The "he said, she said" game is too easily played in that circumstance. Also, we have become masters of incident report documentation. They are generally so detailed that they could be used in a court of law with no questions or room for uncertainty.

Special Occasions and Holidays

When we first opened as a foster home, a board member's wife asked me what we were going to do for the kids' birthdays. You might think I'm crazy, but that never crossed my mind. Fortunately, we have had such a great group of volunteers, they have made our birthday parties as memorable as they can possibly be. A local business pays for each of the birthday cakes, and we find a donor to sponsor the pizzas, sodas, and ice cream. A church thrift store sponsors the decorations. Anywhere from five to fifty volunteers come to celebrate with the kids, making the whole thing seem very festive.

We also find someone to sponsor the cost of the kid's presents, and a volunteer buys and wraps the gifts. At the end of the party, the birthday boy stands up and thanks the attendees for coming. About 50 percent of the time, the kid will say he has never had a birthday celebrated before, and those comments always bring tears. Everyone who has ever come to a Crossroads birthday party has left deeply impacted. A few times, volunteers and board members have brought their own teens to witness the event, and I have heard of more than one quiet and grateful ride home from the party.

I noticed early on that very few of our kids ever got birthday cards in the mail. I brought it up to my own church, and the response was startling. Each of our kids now gets between fifteen and twenty birthday cards, many of which contain money. I have several donors who have sent a handwritten birthday card to every kid who has ever come to Crossroads, some of which are even handmade! Recently, a friend of mine who manages a chiropractic office convinced her chiropractor to buy birthday cards for his patients to sign so that she could send them to the kids. She doubled the number of cards each one of my kids gets!

When I was a teen and received a birthday card, I would check it for money before I read it. Not so with these guys. Of the 480 kids who have been to Crossroads at the date of this writing, I can only remember one kid doing that. I know this because they are required to open the cards in front of me so if they contain money, they write a thank-you card right then and there. Every kid reads every card, some painfully slowly. More often than not, those well wishes from people they have never met end up taped to their bedroom walls. It's an amazing thing. I recently had a thirteen-year-old burst into tears after reading a card. He said he didn't even care that there were ten dollars in the card; he was just amazed a total stranger would say something so nice to him.

One of our board members is really into Halloween. Every year, he donates $1,800 so each of our twenty-four boys can spend seventy-five dollars on their costume. It's humbling to see how thrifty they can be when picking out their costumes. During the week of Halloween, a local business group puts on a costume party for the boys and cooks them a special Halloween meal. On Halloween night we bring the boys into town to go trick-or-treating, and for many of them, it is their first time. It has been such a staple at Crossroads, the kids start asking about it in early September.

For Thanksgiving, each of the staff takes one or two boys home to their own Thanksgiving celebration. Our food service director takes any kids who want to go with her to serve the homeless on Thanksgiving, and she usually has four or five who want to go. For several years I took kids to help serve Thanksgiving dinner at a local church where as many as eight hundred people would come for the holiday meal. It always left an impact on our kids. The community has always been good to us, and we get enough turkeys donated so that each of the staff can have one for their own family celebration.

For our first Christmas, my board chair asked me what we were going to do for the boys. I said I wanted to have each of them sponsored for their presents. He immediately told me he would sponsor them all! I declined because I believed I could find individual families to sponsor each boy. One of the bigger churches in town took that on as a mission, and to date, when anyone asks me about donating for Christmas, I tell them Sacred Heart will likely never give up sponsoring of our boys, partially because of the thank-you notes the boys write back to their sponsors.

On Black Friday, our business manager, Ms. Tina, and her family feverishly shop for our boys after their wish lists have been consolidated. They have done the shopping and wrapping of the Christmas gifts for so long, it has become their family tradition. Tina's family starts coordinating vacations and logistics for the Black Friday event in June. The actual Christmas party has grown so big, we have to celebrate it at a big church in town. Last year we had 160 people come to witness it. A local volunteer couple play Santa and Mrs. Claus, we cater the event, and volunteers decorate for the festivities. Each kid is called up by Santa to receive his gifts, all individually wrapped and contained within a new laundry basket, something they also need. We don't celebrate Christmas for the boys on Christmas Day so we can have the greatest participation by the community. Two other churches provide a small gift and a Christmas stocking for the boys to open on the twenty-fifth, and there is always a group, whether it is a church group or a civic group, who will come out and celebrate with them.

My personal belief is that gifts themselves have no meaning. When someone gives you a thing, the meaning comes from the giving process. For that reason, I sit down with each of the boys after Christmas or their birthday and have them write thank-you cards. This is one of my favorite jobs, and I have learned so much from the kids through the process.

In the beginning, I would correct the kids' grammar and spelling but quickly stopped doing that because I felt the recipient of the card would have a much better understanding when they saw the cards in their raw form. My mom taught me to write thank-you cards when I was growing up, but some of the cards my foster kids have written have literally brought me to tears because of the thought they put into them. By and large, these kids are grateful for the things they get, and they are grateful for being remembered. Their behaviors can be representative of two-year-olds sometimes, but their appreciation comes straight from their hearts. Any caring person easily forgets a kid's transgressions when they witness the kid's appreciation of another person.

A few years ago, a group of local airline flight attendants and personnel started a monthly cultural dinner for our boys. Every third Tuesday they come out to prepare a meal from a different country around the world. They wear costumes and bring costumes for the boys as well. I usually don't get involved in the details when a group or organization wants to plan things with the boys, but when the airlines group brought the boys virgin margaritas for Mexican night, I furled my brow! The kids have made a visible impact on the airlines employees as we see them attend fund-raisers and other functions for Crossroads now too.

Because Charlotte County has some of the best fishing in Florida, we have had several fishing clubs and charter captains take our kids out fishing. One fishing group even put together a fishing tournament where each boat would have one Crossroads kid on board as part of the team. When the COVID-19 pandemic hit, that was put on hold. Most of our kids have never even held a rod, and time spent with the boys fishing can be very impactful on the men teaching them.

If you look on our website, you will see the news articles about a group out of Corpus Christi, Texas, who came to make a documentary about taking one of our kids out fishing. Their assumption was that doing something as simple as taking a boy fishing could make a lasting impact on him. Matthew was recommended for the show by his guardian ad litem and obviously was treated very special by the documentary's film crew and host. He really came into his own after that experience.

For Easter, we usually have a church come and provide services for the kids who want to attend. One church brings Easter baskets for the boys, and another church plans and runs an Easter egg hunt. It is so funny to hear boys say they are too old to sit on the Easter Bunny's lap or run around to find Easter eggs, but when the day of the event comes, those boys are first to line up! Our kids are so deficient in the experiences most of us would consider normal.

About two or three times a year, a donor will pay for all our kids to go to Busch Gardens, the Kennedy Space Center, or somewhere similar. Those trips cost more than $3,000, including transportation, tickets, and meals for twenty-four boys plus staff. They make an impact, though. Almost none of our boys have ever been to an amusement park or a place like the Space Center before, and they come home with wonderment in their eyes. Those places are expensive to visit, but I believe they open the minds of kids to possibility. One of the reasons I became a Navy Diver when I was young was because of the Disney Epcot Center's aquarium called The Living Seas. As an Iowa boy, I never knew how vast and unexplored the ocean was.

Continuation of Operations Plan

If you decide to open a residential facility where multiple lives are at stake, you will need to have a plan for disasters. We call ours a Continuation of Operations Plan (COOP). Within our plan, we have phone trees for notification, supply lists for situations where we may need to take everyone off property, and emergency contact numbers for everyone who would need to be notified of our safety. The plan is updated and trained for annually, and you better believe before hurricane season (June 1) we review the plan with the staff quite seriously. Below are a couple of instances where we actually had to put the COOP plan into practice.

Hurricane Irma

You may not know that in 2004 Hurricane Charlie came up into Charlotte Harbor and created havoc in Charlotte County, Florida. It wasn't predicted to come into Charlotte Harbor originally; it was supposed to head north to Tampa but at the last minute took a right turn. Many Charlotte County residents lost their roofs, and power was out for weeks. Much of Charlotte High School was destroyed to the point portable buildings had to be brought in for teaching and the sports teams had to practice and play in other towns. It took years to rebuild, and obviously people were deeply affected by the whole ordeal.

Hurricane Charlie was a category 4 hurricane. Crossroads, being on the very eastern part of Charlotte County, was fortunate to incur no damage during that event. We ran the campus off our 47-kilowatt generator for two weeks, but other than that, we suffered no consequences. Many staff members' lost the roofs on their homes; some lost their entire homes. Some of Crossroads's "neighbors" brought their refrigerator contents to store in our walk-in freezer. The decision to stay on campus through Hurricane Irma, thirteen years later, was directly because we had fared so well in Charlie.

In September of 2017, category 5 Hurricane Irma was heading directly toward Charlotte County. Most people in Punta Gorda were in all-out panic mode. The prognosticators were painting worst-case scenarios for our community. When the mandatory evacuation order was announced in downtown areas, there was little resistance, as people had a good collective memory of Charlie.

At Crossroads, we developed a staffing plan, and as the storm approached, we moved all the kids and their mattresses into the eight-hundred-square-foot cafeteria. By the time the storm hit, we had barricaded ourselves indoors: seven adults, two dogs, and twenty-one boys. As the front side of the storm hit, we watched through the wire-reinforced glass in the cafeteria's steel door as eighty-foot-tall pine trees were uprooted. For hours we kept the kids busy playing board games and telling jokes while it sounded like a freight train was running across the roof. At one point, I was mesmerized by two boys playing Scrabble with amazing skill and vocabulary.

At a little past 8:00 p.m., the eye of the storm came over the property. Dead calm. We let the kids out to stretch their legs as we had been confined already for five hours. After about twenty minutes, we called them all back in, and shortly after that the back side of the storm began to rage. Tensions were growing among the kids, and a fight broke out between two boys. We had to restrain them for about a half hour until we could get them calmed down. I was pretty mad and disappointed, as we had spent a lot of time mentally preparing the boys for the storm, confinement, and possible aftermath.

By about 1:30 a.m., the storm had all but passed and the winds had calmed down, but it was so dark out, we couldn't assess the property. At 5:00 a.m., I walked out of the cafeteria alone to make sure the property was safe for the kids and shortly after let them and the dogs out. All in all, we lost eight giant trees, one of which smashed in the window of our history classroom, allowing the rain to destroy a bookshelf, some computers, and the carpeting. The roofing was peeled back on three buildings, and one of our basketball goals, cemented in with hundreds of pounds of concrete, was blown over, pulling up the concrete and all. We were without power for two weeks after the storm, but we had prepared by having our thousand-gallon propane tank filled and our generator serviced days before Irma arrived.

The berm around the watermelon field across from Crossroads burst during the night, releasing millions of gallons of retained rainwater across our road. That dug a three-foot-deep trench through our road, making it impossible to get in or out by vehicle.

One of the adults in our group had been updating our status on Facebook, and not long after 5:00 a.m., I got a text from a friend who owns a flooring business saying she would replace all our carpeting in our education building. More people called, texted, and emailed to say they would help. The city of Punta Gorda and most of Charlotte County had received almost no damage to homes, so many of those people turned their attention to Crossroads as the eye of the storm had come directly across our location.

The kids were immensely helpful in the cleanup. Staff got busy notifying case managers and family members their kids were okay. The local builders' association put the word out to its members, so once we got our road opened up, roofers and construction people converged on our campus. Early on, a project coordinator for one of the builders heard the stress in my voice. I had been getting so many phone calls with offers to help, I didn't know how to organize them. She took that load from me and began to work miracles.

One donor from Minneapolis sent a tractor-trailer to us with $18,000 worth of roofing materials. The local Rotary Club brought chainsaws out and cleaned up the debris. A local philanthropic organization put together an emergency fund-raiser and raised $22,000 for us. My board chair commented, "What nonprofit gets destroyed by a hurricane and considers it a blessing?" It took a little over a year to fully recover our facility from the storm, but we were better and stronger for it.

James Lane Allen said, "Adversity does not build character, it reveals it." I think the best part about weathering a trial (pun intended) is that you get to see what you and the people around you are really made of. I wrote in my journal days after Hurricane Irma that I was very proud of the staff and kids for the way they handled the whole crisis.

The day after the storm was over, I decided we would never ride out another hurricane on campus and almost immediately started making contacts in North Carolina where we could move the boys if necessary. In fact, I met with some officials in foster care in November of that year in Charlotte, North Carolina. Later, however, I reconsidered my plan. If you have ever loaded up your family for a week's vacation out of state, think about preparing to move twenty-four boys! The meal planning alone is a daunting task.

On Crossroads's campus, we have full walk-in refrigerators and freezers. Our generator can run for over two weeks on our propane storage and can power the entire campus. Our buildings are rated for hurricanes, and we have full educational and recreational facilities. Moving the kids would mean sleeping bags and constant worries over keeping them busy.

Our COOP plan covers what to do in a hostage situation, a chemical spill, a power outage, a bomb threat, or, as in this case, a hurricane. It's important to have a plan, especially if you have a lot of lives you are responsible for. We also run drills periodically, which makes us more prepared than we would be without them. Having said that, there are things you can't predict, like your only means of egress getting washed out or being confined in a small space for hours on end. To get through those things, you have to be mentally prepared to do whatever it takes and not succumb to feelings of hopelessness or panic.

Coronavirus

When the government announced we were in a worldwide pandemic in the beginning of March 2020, I listened to podcasts about the Spanish flu, or the Great Influenza, and the Black Death to try to understand what the world might look like and how we would need to adapt. I wasn't keen on shutting down the campus and restricting people from coming and going because we relied so heavily on volunteers, but my staff were insistent, so we made the proper notifications. The state of Florida initially forbade public gatherings and shut down parks and all the recreation places we normally took our kids to, so we had to get creative.

Bo, our director of operations, rented a giant inflatable waterslide, and that appeased the kids temporarily. Downtime is bad for anyone but can be dangerous for us with twenty-four boys trying to entertain themselves. This African proverb comes to mind: "If you don't engage the boys, they will burn the village to the ground." Fortunately, the kids accepted isolation like the rest of the world, and we didn't have many incidents until June. We stopped doing intakes of new kids in March because we were afraid we might bring a kid in who had COVID. By mid-April, however, we were down to fourteen boys, and we were concerned about sustainability and running through our savings. Once again, we brought in nine boys in a short amount of time and our incident reports went through the roof. I was very proud of our staff during those first few months in how they handled the kids. I had reminded them in March that we had one seventeen-year-old boy who was immunocompromised and if any of us were careless and brought disease on the campus, it could kill him. God is good. We didn't have a single kid or staff get COVID until June of 2021! By that time, the boy had aged out.

Fund-raising

Admittedly, I have an independent and proud spirit. For those reasons, at least in the beginning, it was exceedingly difficult for me to ask for donations for our mission. It felt as if I was failing and had no choice but to beg for help. I can't remember what caused my change of heart about fund-raising, probably just our sheer need. Not too far into our endeavor,

I realized that for some people contributing to our mission is the only way they can get involved.

Our county, Charlotte County, has one of the oldest average ages per capita in the nation. It is not reasonable for me to expect many of our citizens to come and play basketball with the kids. Those people still want to be a part of what we are doing, though. So, they donate. My mind-set has changed from thinking I was pleading for financial assistance to realizing I'm allowing others to be involved, no matter if their gifts include cooking, playing basketball, or donating resources. To this day, a number of people and churches consider it a privilege to donate monthly to our cause, and we gladly recognize them as partners in our mission—and we're especially gratefully because we have to raise $17,000 per month just to break even.

When we first started out, we focused our fund-raising efforts on events. One of my board members bought a forty-foot inflatable movie screen and projection equipment, and we hosted a monthly drive-in movie in downtown Punta Gorda. That event never made millions, but it brought a lot of exposure to our cause, including volunteers and donations. We also had an annual Sweetheart Ball in February that raised some money but, more importantly, brought friends to our charity.

The biggest impact to our bottom dollar, though, at least in regard to raising funds, is our speaking engagements. I usually take two kids to speak to churches, civic clubs, or other large groups of people at least monthly. Without fail, and without asking, we always walk away with donations and new volunteers from those meetings.

It struck me early on in those speaking engagements that not many people have knowledge about foster care. I learned to ask crowds how many of them had ever been involved in fostering or being fostered. Usually, no hands go up. I then tell the crowd that they, like my wife and I, had probably had a conversation with their spouses at some point about fostering. I would see heads bob in agreement. "But then," I say, "you would have a conversation about the 'Smiths' who had such a terrible experience with fostering." More heads would bob in agreement. "So, you would agree to put off the decision." My closer was, "Well, here's the thing. I am fostering,

I just need your money!" After that, people typically laugh and then line up to give me checks. At one church we walked out with $7,000!

Crossroads also needs in-kind gifts, not just currency. With twelve teen boys in each of the houses, we go through a couch per quarter in each of the great rooms! We put the request in the weekly newsletter and never fail to get a donated couch in response. In many cases, it is easier for people to give in-kind gifts than to write a check. You must be careful, though, and ask the right questions. I once took a donation of a Cadillac that was beautiful inside and out but just needed "a little engine work." When I got the car to my mechanic, he said the aluminum block was cracked and I should just scrap the car for $300. Right after Hurricane Irma, a donor called me and said he wanted to help us out and that he had a big projection TV with a VCR he would like to donate but that we would have to come get it. Keep in mind, this was 2017, not 1997. I told him not even Goodwill would take projection TVs anymore, and he said he had called them and gotten that same message.

The Importance of Volunteers

I cannot overemphasize how important volunteers are in working with foster kids in a group setting. Our experience has been that just by being on-site, volunteers positively affect the culture of both the kids and the staff. It is like having an esteemed guest in your home. The volunteers who have been a part of Crossroads have literally changed kids' lives for the better through their efforts.

When we first opened, I had very little experience working with volunteers. We were not sure how they would work out, but I knew from my pastor friends that you want to choose them carefully because "it's very difficult to fire volunteers!" Unfortunately, over the years I did have to "fire" a few. Fortunately, very few!

One of our longest-term volunteers would come twice per week to tutor a few boys. She was so consistent, she could help new staff learn our processes. About twice per year she would want to meet me in town for breakfast to go over concerns she had that would always have to do with the care of the boys by the staff members. She was so invested that she considered Crossroads to be her own. I learned a lot from her. Unfortunately, she had to move back to her home state after her husband died. She told me that when she went to try to volunteer at a foster home there, they told her the state doesn't allow volunteers to work with foster kids because it is too much of a liability! Wow have they got it wrong.

I've told you about the volunteer mentors we have had and the volunteers who helped with birthdays, Christmas, and other celebrations. They have been invaluable. I don't remember how I met the flight attendant from a local airline who created a monthly themed meal for our boys to celebrate different countries' cultures and heritages, but it is still a major part of the Crossroads programming.

Early on, I advertised for a volunteer event planner since we couldn't afford a resource development person. The woman God brought to me had just retired and was way overqualified for the job. She made light work of setting up our fund-raisers and Christmas parties, organizing volunteers, and making spreadsheets for accountability with the speed and efficiency of a skilled conductor. Her husband joined our board of directors a few years later and still serves on our board to this day.

When speaking to groups, I give examples of my volunteers so people can envision themselves fitting in a role with Crossroads. For many people, especially older people, working with teens seems scary. They often are not sure they can relate. I reassure them, however, that by and large our older volunteers make the biggest impact on the kids since their life experiences easily come through when they spend time with them.

One lady started coming out just to play UNO with a few of the boys. She came weekly, and the kids knew when she was coming and called her Grammy. Eventually, she was able to convince people in her church to build our Crossroads Cantina, which has become a centerpiece for our behavior system and a favorite spot when people come to tour.

Volunteers can be quirky and there is little you can do about that. I have had volunteers walk right into my office when I was at my busiest and sit down across from me to talk. I remind myself in those situations they are a worthwhile investment of time. At one of our first management meetings, we were having a conversation about some of the difficulties of working with volunteers. I asked the group, "Would you rather not have volunteers at Crossroads?" The answer was a unanimous and resounding "No!"

We have a lot of volunteers who work with the boys, and when we were first beginning our endeavor, I walked into the education building to hear a boy cursing angrily in one of the classrooms and banging things around. I walked in and got him calmed down. When I heard there was a volunteer in the library next door who was tutoring a kid, I felt embarrassed and walked over to apologize for the boy's behavior next door. She said, "I grew up with seven brothers. Nothing these kids do is going to faze me!" That was good for me to hear, as there would be plenty more situations like that to come.

What Makes a Good Employee at Crossroads

By and large, people who work in the human services field have to be empathetic toward others. They must also have a high need for intrinsic rewards and a great love for the "underdog" story. If you are reading this book, it is likely those traits describe you and you may think all people are like that. You would be wrong. In the military, I knew plenty of people who had zero empathy for others. This is not necessarily a judgment on my part, as I think there are certain jobs that absolutely require a low level of empathy, unfortunately.

When hiring for positions at Crossroads Hope Academy, I never place value on education. After all, both Jeffrey Skilling and Ted Kaczynski went to Harvard and Jerry Sandusky graduated from Penn State. I wouldn't hire any of those guys to work with my kids! We primarily look for character and for someone who would be a good role model for our boys. We ask all the standard questions in the interview, but those aren't nearly as telling as our "observation day." We ask potential candidates to hang out with our boys for two hours after our school is let out. We observe the potential staff's interactions with the boys and then ask the boys about their opinions of the person. The kids never get it wrong. To a large degree, they have become very savvy in reading people out of a survival necessity. Sometimes, just observing the candidate can be telling. If the person is standoffish or is overtly too involved, that can also be revealing.

Training and Trauma-Informed Care

One of the things we train our staff in is trauma-informed care. They obviously are not equipped to provide psychotherapy to our boys, but understanding behavior through the lens of serious childhood trauma is very effective in how a staff member will deal with that behavior.

Over the last decade, trauma-informed care has become more widely known and used throughout the human services community. The research on the effects of trauma on human development is telling. Permanent physiological changes take place within the brains of the traumatized, affecting emotional and cognitive functioning. This is the most difficult thing to teach new staff and volunteers when they are beginning to interact with our foster kids.

By and large, most foster kids are emotionally deregulated due to their traumatic experiences. If your own kid were to scream out in church or in a quiet gathering, you probably would be furious and embarrassed and react to those feelings. For foster kids, however, you can't assume they are consciously and intentionally being disruptive in that example. There could be much deeper and more basic operations happening that are causing that child to cry out.

As a practitioner, it is important to know some details on each of the kids to know how to avoid their triggers. But there are also universal practices in working with people who have been traumatized so you don't inadvertently retraumatize them. For example, about 90 percent of our boys have been sexually abused in some manner. It isn't forbidden for the staff to touch or hug the kids, but there are some ground rules. You wouldn't want to sneak up behind a person who has been traumatized sexually and surprise them with a slap on the back. You might get punched in that situation. Further, your actions might retraumatize a kid who likewise did not foresee the unwanted physical advance of an adult in their life whom they'd previously trusted. Your action may cause them to relive the experience.

Moving too quickly around a person who has been physically abused might cause them to flinch. Though your intentions weren't bad, your lack of understanding might cause an escalation in behavior in that person, causing further emotional and physical stress. Being consistent and pre-dictable in your behavior while working with people who have endured trauma will help build trust, the foundation of relationship.

We provide about fifty hours of training to our new staff before they interact with the kids. They train in Handle with Care, a program that teaches de-escalation techniques both verbally and physically, CPR and First Aid, and a host of other topics. Annually, our staff get training in about forty-five hours of training topics, including knowledge of human trafficking and dealing with trafficking victims.

Get Involved

Every state in the nation, and every nation in the world, has a shortage of people who are willing to foster kids. I'm hoping that throughout this book I have demystified some of your concerns if you are considering fos-tering. Based on my conversations over the years, I am confident there are many people willing to take foster kids in if they could count on support. If you are going to foster, you will need it.

A friend of mine runs a global organization called Patch Our Planet. He helps churches develop orphan care strategies so that foster families are fully supported to carry out that role. Some people help babysit so foster parents can go out for date nights. Some help with food, some with clothes, and some with driving to appointments.

You may not be able to foster, but you can help. I will tell you, as one who is fostering, I don't think I could ever get too much support at Crossroads.

Chapter 11

The Future of Crossroads

Santonio

S antonio had aged out of foster care four months earlier. While he lived at Crossroads, he was one of our most responsible kids and tried to be a big brother to many. This day, he came back to talk to the staff and kids at Crossroads. He specifically sought out a boy named Daniel, whom he had been friends with and who would also be aging out within weeks.

"It's not what you think," he told Daniel. "Nobody is going to be there to get you up and make sure you are being responsible once you are eighteen. If you don't take care of your business, you'll be homeless." Daniel wasn't hearing it. He was like every other eighteen-year-old we had seen with an attitude of "it won't happen to me." Unfortunately, Daniel didn't take care of his responsibilities and was homeless within two months of aging out.

This final chapter is being written on the eve of our expansion of Crossroads Hope Academy. In fact, my board made a motion just yesterday to go under contract on a fifteen-thousand-square-foot building in the heart of Punta Gorda. By the end of 2022, it looks as if we will be bringing in another twenty-four boys and twenty staff members to that location.

We receive an average of eighty referrals for placement per month, so I'm not concerned about getting kids. We got a call yesterday from a placing agency who had thirteen teen boys in their offices. They had no place for them to go. He had to tell them we were full and have a waiting list. My concern is not with placements but with hiring.

As the pandemic has begun to subside, most businesses are struggling to hire. Our background check requirements add a level of difficulty in bringing on new staff. Most importantly, however, is that we want to have the right role models for our boys. All I can do is trust God to bring the right people to us.

The operational plan with the new building will be that we will bring all new kids to our current site. The kids who behave well will be allowed to move into town where it will be easier to hang out with friends and work a job. We are hoping the kids will see the opportunity as an incentive to get and keep their behaviors under control.

Doubling our population in a year is obviously nerve-racking for me. We want to be able to take in more kids to keep them off the streets and out of runaway shelters, and we obviously believe we have a good model for working with the kind of teens we work with. Still, I'm concerned about stressing the resources of some of our stakeholders: the sheriff's department, the school district, and the local mental health agency where the kids who Baker Act themselves go. I suppose, just like you, I have to keep Matthew 6:34 in mind. Jesus said, "Do not worry about tomorrow, for tomorrow will worry about itself. Each day has enough trouble of its own" (NIV).

In chapter 7, I talked about having a consistent place where our eighteen-and-up population can live and thrive. In recent months there have been some developments on that as well. A local friend of mine wrote and won a federal grant that specifically addresses homelessness among the eighteen-to-twenty-four-year-old population. We have had a lot of communication recently about how that might benefit our boys once they age out.

I haven't taken my eyes off North Carolina either. When I met with the officials in foster care there, they said they could absolutely use us to help with their teen population. I think most if not all states would welcome the help. Selfishly, I would love to be able to see my grandkids more often and they live in Charlotte. "Many are the plans in the mind of a man, but it is the purpose of the LORD that will stand" (Proverbs 19:21). I will wait upon Him and take this one step at a time.

Epilogue

Nate had been with us for over two years. He was flying to Indiana to finish high school and live with his grandparents. Through all his excitement of packing and getting last-minute documents from Ms. Charity, he stopped, put everything down, and came in to say, "Mr. John, thank you for not giving up on me." I teared up, of course, and then gave him a hug.

Caleb was going to go back to live with his father who had just gotten out of jail. The father told the caseworker he wasn't ready for the responsibility yet, but they sent thirteen-year-old Caleb to him anyway. We were all concerned. I wasn't there when they came to pick him up, but when I came in the next day, he had placed on my desk a wooden sign he'd made in the vocational shop that read "FAITH"; it had a note on it that said, "Goodbye Mr. John, Love Caleb." That sign still sits on my shelf where I can read it daily, seven years later. I pray that he is okay.

Demetrious was a very big fifteen-year-old. His anger was quick, and he didn't calm down for an hour usually after he got mad. But he had a sweet side, too, and would hug on and talk to other kids when they were struggling. One day someone pushed his buttons just right, and it took both my team leader and me to restrain him so he wouldn't hurt anyone or himself. After holding him for what seemed like forever, he burst into tears and sobbed, "Why don't my parents want me? Why doesn't anyone want me?" My heart hurt for him, and just typing this is bringing me to tears thinking about it. We live in a truly fallen world if parents can abandon their own children.

I could tell you a hundred other similar stories. Fostering kids can be excruciatingly difficult sometimes. I've lost countless hours of sleep over the years. I want so badly to fix my kids' lives sometimes that it makes me crazy thinking about who to fight to get justice for them. There have been a few times I have been curled up in a ball on my bed in heavy depression over the torn and broken lives I deal with on a daily basis. But I honestly can't imagine there is anything else I would rather be doing with my life. I never go home at the end of the day and wonder if I am making a difference.

I would be remiss if I didn't tell you that if you choose to get involved in fostering, make sure you assess the reason you are doing so, and be prepared to have your heart broken. It will happen if you are at all human. Only a handful of the kids who have left Crossroads over the years have reached out to us. We reach out to them from time to time, at least the ones we can find, but most of our former kids have moved on with their lives. We can only hope that we have positively impacted them and helped prepare them in their life's journey.

I recently heard a story about foster parents whose seventeen-year-old foster daughter declared that she wanted to be emancipated and just picked up and moved to Georgia. They raised her for the last seven years, took her to England, helped her become a "ball girl" for the US Women's Tennis Association, and provided her with a loving and secure home. The foster parents were heartbroken. The husband literally became so depressed he got sick. They have not even heard from her since she left. I wish I could tell you that is a unique story, but actually it is more the norm when dealing with foster kids. They may leave your home and never look back. I'm telling you in order to prepare you for when it happens. Again, make sure you are fostering for the right reason.

James 1:27 says we are to look after orphans. In Matthew 5:44, Jesus tells us to love our enemies. A synonym for *enemy* is "adversary," and anyone who has raised teens or two-year-olds will agree that at times those are adversarial relationships.

If this book has caused you hesitation in fostering kids or even "visiting orphans," that was not my intention. Please reach out to me. Give me the chance to change your mind. If God has put foster kids on your heart, then do not fear. Join the battle. Foster kids need you.

To find out more about Crossroads Hope Academy or to donate to our mission, please visit www.CrossroadsPG.org or www.FaceBook.com/crossroadshopeacademy.

You can also contact me, the executive director at Crossroads, at John@CrossroadsPG.org or call our office at 941.575.5790.

If you would like to be added to our weekly e-newsletter, please email Liz Green at Liz@CrossroadsPG.org.

If you would like to find out more about how your church can get involved with foster care, please contact Pastor Steve Gillis at Steve@PatchOurPlanet.org or go to www.PatchOurPlanet.org.

About the Author

I am often asked how I got into the work of foster care. My initial response is that it is not what I had planned to do professionally! Let me also dispel the myth that there is some appropriate training to be qualified to parent behaviorally difficult teen foster boys. I get the question about qualifications quite often, and my answer has become "If God didn't appoint me to do this job, I wouldn't be doing it!"

After six years in the world's finest navy as an Explosive Ordnance Disposal Diver, my plan was to go to medical school. Going to EOD school was both physically and mentally demanding, and I figured if I could handle that, I could handle medical school. I began down that path after getting out of the navy. But after a simple prayer, prayed on the back of a French tugboat in the Mediterranean Sea, God decided to be funny and set me on a path working with juvenile offenders in the juvenile justice system. I was a natural at that job, and I found it very fulfilling. I've got to tell you, though: it took all of the discipline that I'd gained in the military and everything I learned in the eighteen years I spent with juvenile delinquents to weather the storms I have faced thus far in foster care!

In the navy, I learned self-discipline. I learned how to lean in when things got tough. In the juvenile justice world, I learned how to be a disciplinarian and develop the strengths in others. Those attributes have positives and negatives. On the one hand, for a person who has learned a great deal of self-discipline, it can be frustrating to work with people who have none. Yes, opposites attract, but you can only try to convince someone to stop beating his head on the wall so many times before you want to beat your own head on the wall. On the other hand, discipline is exactly what kids need to succeed in life beyond parental control so there is no giving up, something else the military taught me.

I will also say that my biological kids were grown and out of the house when we turned Crossroads over to a foster home and school. Had I known then what I know now, my parenting would probably have looked a little different as well. I suppose all parents could utter those words though as "hindsight is always 20/20".

I have three grown kids of my own who are thankfully all doing very well for themselves. Praise God! I also have three grandchildren, triplets, who I absolutely adore. My wife and I travel as often as we can, and we enjoy seeing live music together whenever we can, however, my mind is never far from Crossroads.